AF334159

# A PARENT'S GUIDE

## TO

# High Stakes Testing

A PARENT'S GUIDE

# TO

# High Stakes Testing

*Edith N. Wagner*

NEW YORK

Copyright © 2002 LearningExpress, LLC.

All rights reserved under International and Pan-American Copyright Conventions.
Published in the United States by LearningExpress, LLC, New York.

Library of Congress Cataloging-in-Publication Data:
Wagner, Edith N.
    A parent's guide to high stakes testing / Edith Wagner.—1st ed.
        p. cm.
    ISBN 1-57685-417-5 (pbk.)
    1. Educational tests and measurements—United States—Handbooks,
manuals, etc.  2. Education—Standards—United States—Handbooks,
manuals, etc.  I. Title.
    LB3051 .W26 2002
    371.26'4—dc21

                                                          2002003609

Printed in the United States of America
9 8 7 6 5 4 3 2 1
First Edition

ISBN 1-57685-417-5

For more information or to place an order, contact LearningExpress at:
    900 Broadway
    Suite 604
    New York, NY 10003

Or visit us at:
    www.learnatest.com

ABOUT THE AUTHORS

**Edith N. Wagner** is the author of *Basic Skills for College* and *Express Yourself: Writing Skills for High School*. A former English teacher, she is now a college instructor and writer living in Knoxville, Tennessee.

**Jessika Sobanski**, contributor of the math sections in this book, is a math and test preparation instructor and writer from Long Island, New York.

# CONTENTS

**P**art of the common values we share as a democratic society is that basic literacy skills are as fundamental as food and shelter. We provide mandatory public education for our children and we pride ourselves on preparing them as future citizens of the world. In the late 1950s our confidence in public education was shaken when Russia launched Sputnik. We found it hard to believe that the United States, with its emphasis on education and excellence, would be surpassed by the Soviet Union. It was the first time in the history of our public education that we began to doubt ourselves and national attention was quickly focused on improving education.

To that end, money was poured into math and science programs, and teacher training efforts were redoubled. But events like the Vietnam War and the Women's and Civil Rights Movements took hold of America's consciousness in the late sixties and early seventies and the spotlight shifted away from education. It was not until the early eighties that our classrooms again came under serious scrutiny. In 1983, *A Nation at Risk* was presented to the American people. It was an alarming study of our educational system and it concluded that our children were not being educated to meet the needs of an increasingly technological workplace and global community. Standardized tests, administered internationally, found that American students were seriously behind other nations in subjects such as math, science, and geography. The call went out. States were to reinvigorate their programs, upgrade their curricula, retrain their teachers, and *make sure that children were learning more and better.*

Since 1983 and the first publication of *A Nation at Risk*, it has been the last part of that equation that has been the biggest challenge. Just how does a school system, whether in Arkansas or Alaska, *make sure that children learn more and better?* Traditionally, states have control over what curricula their schools follow, and traditionally, individual school systems, right down to your neighborhood school, respond to the unique demands of their communities. Local control has been a fundamental right of public schools because it is local dollars that drive the services that schools provide. It is very difficult to provide common services when there are not common dollars. Yet, *A Nation at Risk* put all of America's schools on notice that there was an urgent need to rethink our common educational priorities. Specifically, our children had to be able to demonstrate that they could meet clearly delineated goals in the major academic areas of English/Language Arts, mathematics, science, and social studies. The need for second language instruction, health education, attention to art and music, athletics and business education, not to mention computer literacy and library/media skills, were also to be upgraded, but it was the "big four" that were to be the benchmarks for success.

To begin the task of ensuring that our nation's common purposes in education were being addressed, there was an effort on the part of each of the states to redefine its local needs in terms of this national educational agenda. Following are excerpts from various state documents, which have been developed in response to the need for strengthened educational standards.

> ▶ The mission of the North Carolina public school community is to challenge, with high expectations, each child to learn, to achieve, and to fulfill his or her potential. To encourage a strong academic emphasis on the basic skills (reading, writing, and mathematics) that all students should master. *North Carolina ABCs of Public Education*

> ▶ Delaware students must meet world-class standards if they are to be competitive and successful in a global economy. To prepare our children for their future, our schools must support rigorous standards and each of our teachers must set high expectations. Our students should commit themselves to the achievement of excellence. *Delaware Department of Education Student Testing Program Introduction*

▶ By the end of grade 12, students will develop proficiency, confidence and fluency in reading, writing, listening, speaking, and viewing to meet the literacy demands of the twenty-first century. Students will apply proficiently a range of numerical, algebraic, geometric, and statistical concepts and skills to formulate, analyze, and solve real-world problems; to facilitate inquiry and the exploration of real-world phenomena; and to support continued development and appreciation of mathematics as a discipline.
*Connecticut State Department of Education program goals for Language Arts and Mathematics*

▶ To succeed in the next century, today's young people will be expected to know more and have higher-level skills than any previous generation. Schools are raising academic expectations, building a firm foundation from the basics and ensuring the higher-level skills demanded by the modern workplace and higher education.
*Maryland State Department of Education High School Improvement Program*

Common words and phrases peppered state documents from coast to coast: global economy, technological workplace, appreciation of mathematics, ability to communicate effectively, ability to collaborate with others, more rigorous learning, ability to problem solve, and the list goes on. The common call became more clear. Higher expectations and higher performance standards were needed to ensure that our children were being prepared for the rigorous demands of the twenty-first century global marketplace.

## The Stakes Are Very High

IT HAS BECOME increasingly clear that the stakes riding on educating our children are very high. As technology shrinks our world, as business demands more sophisticated communication skills, and as our economy becomes more dependent on our partners overseas, our nation, and our families, will rely more on our schools to provide the means for us to compete and succeed.

As parents and taxpayers, you are probably wondering where you fit into this national dialogue. You may feel that you were adequately prepared in school and you may be perfectly satisfied with the schools your children attend. Or, you may be very concerned that your children are being shortchanged. You may feel that they are not coming home with enough homework or that the demands being made are too severe. This book will attempt to answer some of your questions. Specifically, just how is your state answering the call for reform? Just where does your school district fit into this picture? Just what is your local elementary, middle, or high school doing to prepare your child for your state's new demands? What is your state demanding, anyway? And, perhaps most important, just what can *you* do to help your child rise to these new demands?

## How to Use This Book

YOU HEAR IT all the time. Parents must get *involved* with their children. From that first PTA or PA meeting, you are told that an active role is needed, wanted, and is vital to your child's success in school. But have you ever been told how to get involved? Sure, you sign up for the bake sales and you answer the calls to volunteer for field trips and fundraisers. You put your name on every list and attend every function. But by the time middle school rolls around, and certainly by high school, the requests for your participation become fewer and fewer and you become less and less certain just how to support the academic mission of your child's school. Did you even know that there was such a mission and that it is probably posted in the entryway of the school building? Let's look at two mission statements.

> ▶ Our students meet or exceed set academic standards, accept responsibility
>    for their conduct, character, and achievement, and successfully make the
>    transition to post-secondary challenges.
>    *Catoctin Senior High School, Maryland*

> ▶ Farragut High School will provide a challenging curriculum in an en-
>    vironment conducive to learning that will enable students to become
>    knowledgeable, creative, and ethical contributors to a diverse society.
>    *Farragut High School, Tennessee*

Like the vision statements set by the district, the individual school your child attends also has a vision, or a mission, which states the broad goals for your child's success. Most of these statements are nothing with which anyone could argue, but you must probe more deeply and find out what the school offers your child in the way of programs, courses, remediation, tutoring, counseling, and extra-curricular activities to achieve these goals.

This book is intended to give you information about the state assessments (tests) that your child will take in elementary, middle, and high school. These tests are a critical part of the academic mission of your child's education because they are designed to measure his or her grade level abilities to determine whether or not he or she is meeting the academic standards set, not just by the school, but by your State Department of Education. As of this writing, every state has, or is well on its way to establishing exit examination requirements in the four "big" academic areas: English/Language Arts, mathematics, science, and social studies. The term "exit" means exams that your child must pass in order to earn a high school diploma. And as of this writing, President Bush has signed into federal law the requirement that all states administer yearly testing for elementary and middle school children. (See Chapter 1 for further discussion of this important development.)

Simply put, the academic mission that every child will demonstrate competence at a significantly higher level in English/Language Arts, math, science, and social studies is translated into whether or not he or she can pass a test to prove it. And you really do have to get involved and help. This book will:

- ▶ explain the concepts and contents of the new tests.
- ▶ provide sample question types with answers and explanations.
- ▶ provide practice questions.
- ▶ provide tips for helping you help your child succeed.
- ▶ examine the new *No Child Left Behind* bill and show how it may directly affect you and your children.

*Chapter 1* discusses how vague expectations for "higher standards," "more rigorous performance," "boosting confidence," and "communicating effectively" are actually translated into performance goals that can be measured.

*Chapter 2* discusses the actual tests, which your children will take to determine their grade level abilities to meet those performance standards. Specific attention will be given to the English/Language Arts and mathematics tests, which are part of every school district's elementary, middle, and high school assessment program. Social studies and science assessments will also be mentioned.

*Chapter 3* provides guidance for the high school English/Language Arts assessments (tests).

*Chapter 4* provides guidance for the high school mathematics assessments (tests).

*Chapter 5* provides guidance for the middle school English/Language Arts assessments (tests).

*Chapter 6* provides guidance for the middle school mathematics assessments (tests).

*Chapter* 7 provides guidance for the elementary school English/Language Arts assessments (tests).

*Chapter 8* provides guidance for the elementary school mathematics assessments (tests).

*Chapter 9* discusses specific strategies to help you become a more involved participant in your child's academic career and the *No Child Left Behind* legislation signed into law on January 8, 2002, is more fully explored.

*Appendix A* provides a state-by-state list of websites for easy access to your state's specific tests and administration dates as well as scoring keys.

*Appendix B* provides a list of suggested further reading for you and your child.

A PARENT'S GUIDE

TO

# High Stakes Testing

# Translating Expectations into Performance Standards

**B**efore we go any further, you need a crash course in *educationese*. That's the language of education, which can be very confusing. For example, you may have noticed that back in the introduction, the word *tests* was in parentheses after the word *assessments*. That's because very few tests are given anymore. They are now called assessments because unlike old-fashioned tests that were designed for right or wrong answers to very content specific questions, the new tests also measure the process students use to arrive at an answer or explanation, not just the answer itself. Think of it as process versus product. The traditional test scored the product—the answer. The assessment scores the process—thinking as well as answers.

Following is a list of terms which have become part of the vocabulary of the new reform movement in education:

*Academic standards* are clearly defined statements of what students are expected to know and be able to do.

*Content standards* describe the knowledge and skills of a particular content area—such as social studies or science—that students should learn. Content standards specify the concepts and knowledge essential to the content area.

*Performance standards* are concrete examples of what students should be able to do to demonstrate that they have not only learned but understand and are able to apply the content they have learned. Unlike content standards, which specify what students should know, performance standards specify how students should be able to use content knowledge, often in real world situations.

*Benchmarks* are points of reference, often a score or satisfactory accomplishment of a task or set of tasks, to demonstrate a masterful performance. Benchmarks represent detailed sets of knowledge and/or measures of performance expected of students at a given age, grade, or developmental level.

*Assessment* is the process by which the achievement, aptitude, or knowledge of a student or group of students is measured. There are different types of assessment. The traditional short answer test is one type of assessment, much less frequently used than alternative or authentic assessments that ask students to demonstrate how they apply knowledge and skills, often in real world situations.

*Norm-referenced scoring* is the grading of student work compared to "the norm group." Students can fall below the norm, at the norm, or above the norm because the norm has been pre-set. Standardized tests such as the Stanford Achievement Test or the Iowa Test of Basic Skills are examples of norm-referenced tests. In the past, school districts relied on these standardized tests much more heavily than they do today or will in the future. Now, states are redesigning their curricula and their testing programs to reflect their own very specific academic standards.

*Criterion referenced scoring* is the grading of student work against a set of specific criteria. Unlike norm-referenced scoring, when a class set of papers is scored against a set of criteria, everyone can achieve very high or very low scores. There is no "norm" or middle ground to gauge whether or not a student has scored above or below. For example, criterion referencing is used to grade writing samples.

*Standards based criterion-referenced assessments* are a way of putting it all together. These are assessments (tests) that measure a student's attainment of specific academic standards, using question types that require more than just the right or wrong answers. These assessments generally require the writing of explanations or the demonstration of the process(es) used to arrive at an answer. Most, if not all, new state assessments are standards based criterion-referenced.

Before you throw your hands up in despair, look on the bright side of things. At least now you have some basic understanding of what kind of tests your child will be taking. And that takes us right back to the content standards.

## Content Standards

THE FIRST IMPORTANT documents that you should want to know more about are the various content standard descriptions that are written by your state education department curriculum offices. For instance, in New York State you would want to have Learning Standards for English Language Arts that carefully explain the goals for English/Language Arts instruction in that state. A document such as this is intended primarily for the state's educators to guide them in developing school district and individual school programs. However, these documents provide valuable insight into just what your child's teachers should be addressing in their daily instructional programs—because these documents are blueprints for that state's testing program.

Copies of these documents can be obtained by asking your school district's central office assistant superintendent of curriculum, your child's principal, or by going directly to your state's website. (A list of state websites is given in Appendix A.) Remember, you are asking for your state's content standards by subject area. You should be able to receive English/Language Arts, mathematics, science, social studies, second languages, health, art, and music. Start with just the big four because these are the ones that drive the accountability testing for your child.

Once you have a copy of the document, start by looking at the general learning (academic) standards for that content area. Let's use New York's English/Language Arts (ELA) standard description as a model. This document breaks down the goals for ELA into four parts:

> ▶ Students will read, write, listen, and speak for information and understanding. As listeners and readers, students will collect data, facts, and ideas; discover relationships, concepts, and generalizations; and use knowledge generated from oral, written, and electronically produced texts. As speakers and writers, they will use oral and written language to acquire, interpret, apply, and transmit information.

▶ Students will read, write, listen, and speak for literary response and expression. Students will read and listen to oral, written, and electronically produced texts and performances, relate texts and performances to their own lives, and develop an understanding of the diverse social, historical, and cultural dimensions the texts and performances represent. As speakers and writers, students will use oral and written language for self-expression and artistic creation.

▶ Students will read, write, listen, and speak for critical analysis and evaluation. As listeners and readers, students will analyze experiences, ideas, information, and issues presented by others using a variety of established criteria. As speakers and writers, they will present, in oral and written language and from a variety of perspectives, their opinions and judgments on experiences, ideas, information, and issues.

▶ Students will read, write, listen, and speak for social interaction. Students will use oral and written language for effective social communication with a wide variety of people. As readers and listeners, they will use the social communications of others to enrich their understanding of people and their views.

You will notice that these are very broad goals or *learning standards*. They apply to elementary, middle, and high schoolers equally. Obviously, they need to be broken down and made more specific. This is where *performance standards* come into play. What would a second grader have to *do* to demonstrate that he or she can listen and read for information and understanding? One suggested indication that a second grader has listened for information and understanding would be his or her ability to accurately paraphrase a story just heard or read, or to follow directions that involve more than one step. Broken down yet further, can your second grader paraphrase *The Little Engine That Could*, including details of time and place?

The tip below is one way to use the state curriculum document to help your child at home. You can talk to your child's teacher very specifically about the strategies you are using at home and ask if there are other, better, ways for you to be spending time with your child supporting the skills that are being developed in school.

> ☛ **PARENT TIP:** When you read to your elementary schooler, ask him or her to retell the story and direct him or her to remember when, where, and why.

Another way that the state documents can help you is that many will provide examples of what competent work should look like. We all think our children are doing well. Sometimes it is very helpful to see what others at the same age are capable of.

Remember how you used your Dr. Spock books to gauge early walking, talking, and eating behaviors? Well, why not evaluate your fifth grader's writing ability in response to literature against other fifth graders? Again, New York State's English/Language Arts document does a good job of offering samples of student work.



Performance standards used to evaluate this task are:

Students will be able to:

▶ recognize some features that distinguish the genres.
▶ create their own stories, poems, and songs, using the elements of the literature they have read and with appropriate vocabulary.
▶ observe the conventions of grammar, usage, spelling, and punctuation.

Is this a good response for a fifth grader? The state document evaluates it this way:

> ▶ It demonstrates knowledge of the narrative form, with a lead that provides an immediate entry to the story, use of storytelling language such as "one day," a conversational style, and a circular structure that connects the ending with ideas expressed earlier in the text.
> ▶ It uses chronological order, an acceptable narrative structure.
> ▶ It reveals use of language for a particular effect; that is, to describe the main character's anxiety and the change in her feelings from the beginning of the day to the end.
> ▶ It shows control over basic language conventions—including correct spelling, punctuation, and use of commas in a series—as well as varied and complex sentence structures.

In other words, the sample is a good example of what a fifth grade student should be able to produce in response to a task designed to measure his or her use of language for response to literature.

> ☞ **PARENT TIP:** A good teaching technique is to show a model or sample of an assignment to make expectations clear. If your child is not achieving the grades you think are correct, ask to see a sample of what is considered to be an age and grade appropriate response. Then you and your child's teacher can help figure out what you can do at home to help your child practice more effectively.

Most of the curriculum documents from the various state departments of education are arranged to offer specific examples of performance tasks with exemplars (examples of student work) to demonstrate exactly what can be expected at grade and age appropriate levels of performance. These can be very helpful to you in understanding exactly where you child fits on the performance scale.

Now let's take a look at the way the Ohio Department of Education has outlined its Mathematics Contents Standards. They are listed as:

> ▶ *Numbers, Number Sense, and Operations*
> Students demonstrate number sense including an understanding of number systems and of operations, and how they relate to one another. Students compute fluently and make reasonable estimates using paper and pencil, technology supported, and mental methods.

- ▶ *Measurement*

  Students estimate and measure to a required degree of accuracy and precision by selecting and using appropriate units, tools, and technologies.

- ▶ *Geometry and Spatial Sense*

  Students identify, classify, compare, and analyze characteristics, properties and relationships of one-, two-, and three-dimensional geometric figures and objects. Students use spatial reasoning, properties of geometric objects, and transformations to analyze mathematical situations and solve problems.

- ▶ *Patterns, Functions, and Algebra*

  Students use patterns, relations, and functions to model, represent, and analyze problem situations that involve quantities. Students analyze, model, and solve problems using various representations such as tables, graphs, and equations.

- ▶ *Data Analysis and Probability*

  Students pose questions and collect, organize, represent, interpret, and analyze data to answer those questions. Students develop and evaluate inferences, predictions, and arguments that are based on data.

- ▶ *Mathematical Processes*

  Students use mathematical processes and knowledge to solve problems. Students apply problem-solving and decision-making techniques, and communicate mathematical ideas.

But as you already know, content standards are just the beginning. A very comprehensive document titled "K-12 Mathematics" was prepared by representatives from all twelve regions served by the Ohio Department Regional Professional Development Centers, including educators from each grade level, K-12, as well as career-technical, special education, and gifted education, plus parent, business and industry representatives. The content standards are given depth and breadth and translated into very specific grade-level performance standards, indicators, and benchmarks. For example, in Ohio, parents can expect that by the end of grade two their children will be able to do the following:

### Numbers and Number Systems Indicators for Grade Two

1. Use place value concepts to represent, compare, and order whole numbers using physical models, numerals, and words, with ones, tens, and hundreds. For example:

   a. Recognize 10 can mean "10 ones" or a single entity (1 ten) through physical models and trading games.

b. Read and write three-digit numerals (e.g., 243 as two hundred forty-three, 24 tens and 3 ones, or 2 hundreds and 43 ones, etc.) and construct models to represent each.

2. Recognize and classify numbers as even or odd.
3. Count money and make change using coins and a dollar bill.
4. Represent and write the value of money using the $ and ¢ signs and in decimal form when using the $ sign.
5. Represent fractions (halves, thirds, fourths, sixths, and eighths), using words, numerals, and physical models. For example:
   a. Recognize that a fractional part can mean different amounts depending on the original quantity.
   b. Recognize that a fractional part of a rectangle does not have to be shaded with continuous parts.
   c. Identify and illustrate parts of a whole and parts of sets of objects.
   d. Compare and order physical models of halves, thirds, and fourths in relation to 0 and 1.

### Meaning of Operations Indicators for Grade Two

6. Model, represent, and explain subtraction as comparison, take-away, and part-to-the-whole; for example, solve missing addend problems by counting up or subtracting, such as, "I had six baseball cards, my sister gave me more, and I now have ten. How many did she give me?" can be represented as $6 + ? = 10$ or $10 - 6 = ?$
7. Model, represent, and explain multiplication as repeated addition, rectangular arrays, and skip counting.
8. Model, represent, and explain division as sharing equally and repeated subtraction.
9. Model and use the commutative property for addition.

### Computation and Estimation Indicators for Grade Two

10. Demonstrate fluency in addition facts with addends through 9 and corresponding subtractions; for example, $9 + 9 = 18$, $18 - 9 = 9$.
11. Add and subtract multiples of 10.
12. Demonstrate multiple strategies for adding and subtracting two- or three-digit whole numbers, such as:
    a. Compatible numbers
    b. Compensatory numbers
    c. Informal use of commutative and associative properties of addition
13. Estimate the results of whole number addition and subtraction problems using front-end estimation and judge the reasonableness of the answers.

Notice how there are some very definite tasks spelled out to give life to the general content standards. A performance task that a classroom teacher might use to teach and then measure the accomplishment of one of these standards might be to set up a small store in the classroom and watch as the children buy and sell and make appropriate change to demonstrate their "ability to count money and make change using coins and a dollar bill." This real-world simulation would also measure their ability to represent fractions as they divide whatever merchandise they might offer for sale, such as cookies.

☛ **PARENT TIP:** Have your child practice fractions by dividing the food on his or her plate into halves and thirds.

The Ohio document is very similar to the mathematics curriculum documents of each of the 50 states. All have written or are in the process of writing extensive manuals to spell out very clearly what students should be able to know and do to be accomplished citizens of our highly technological and competitive world. The purpose of these efforts is clear: accountability.

## THE ACCOUNTABILITY ISSUE

As mentioned in the introduction, on Tuesday, January 8, 2002, President George W. Bush signed into legislation the most comprehensive federal school legislation since the Elementary and Secondary Education Act of 1965. The bill, H.R. 1, the *No Child Left Behind Act*, contains numerous provisions to help states use federal funds to raise standards and ensure that America's underserved children, those from low-income families, are given comparable educational opportunities as students from more affluence. The bill's primary purpose is to provide federal muscle to the task of raising America's educational accomplishments, and ensuring that *all* of her children are adequately prepared for social and economic success in the twenty-first century.

Among the bill's provisions is the plan to hold state and local school districts that use federal funds *accountable* for improving student achievement by requiring annual reading and math assessments in grades three through eight. Although its primary emphasis is on reading instruction, specifically supporting phonics instruction as the "scientifically based" way to teach reading, the bill also includes provisions for empowering parents, making schools safer, improving math and science education, promoting English fluency, and improving teacher quality. But at issue for our purposes is the *accountability* part.

There are many people who have a stake in public education. Children rely on teachers to provide basic skills and to open the doors of advanced educational opportunity.

Teachers rely on administrators to provide the materials and resources to help them. Adminstrators rely on local boards of education, local business, and community leadership for funds and support. School districts need state funding to subsidize local funds. States need the federal government, and the interconnectivity goes on and on. But no individual or group wants to keep pouring resources, whether money or confidence, into programs that don't work. So how do you demonstrate success? How do you hold local districts *accountable* for the sometimes multimillion dollar expenditures of their communities? How do you hold teachers *accountable* for teaching children basic skills? How do you hold building principals *accountable* for creating learning conditions that ensure success? How do you hold parents *accountable* for sending children to school ready to learn?

The accountability issue is huge and amorphous, but with billions of dollars on the table, and the future of our country and children at stake, the education community has tackled the issue head on. Accountability had to be made tangible, and test results, along with measurability, became the first piece of the puzzle. H.R. 1, the *No Child Left Behind Act*, recognized and legitimized this when it required testing for grades three through eight to gauge success.


## How Do You Measure Success?

YOUR STATE MAY already require that your local school district publish an annual report card. The purpose of this document, which reports your local school's test scores from whatever standardized tests your state requires, is to give you information about the successes or failures of your local school compared with others in your community. Casting public attention in this way holds your individual school accountable to you for the services that it is providing to your child. More importantly, though, this accountability is reinforcing your invitation to get involved. *Your individual school does not want to be at the bottom of any state lists!*

However, your local school doesn't want to be, nor should it be, held totally responsible for its failures. Parents love to bask in a school's glory. We love to be partners in success. But we cannot take credit only for success. We have to accept responsibility for failure as well. Therefore, you must look at your school's report card as an invitation for you to become involved, to accept your piece of the accountability puzzle.

The traditional invitations are extended to you through parents associations, school board meetings, extracurricular activities, performances, and fund-raisers, to name a few. But we are not talking about traditional responsibilities anymore. We are talking about your high stakes accountability for your child's academic achievement. Yes, you should keep going to parents association meetings. Of course you should support the band trips and the candy sales. But you must also become much more knowledgeable about how to measure your child's learning progress.

## Performance Goals That Can Be Measured

LET'S GO BACK to those New York State English/Language Arts Standards and the Ohio Mathematics Standards. Do you see now why so much attention is being paid to creating very specific language to identify what students need to know and exactly how to determine if they know it? It isn't sufficient to say we want our children to be *good* readers. We have to define *good* and then define how to measure *good*. It isn't enough to say that we want our children to be *mathematically literate*. We have to know what that means in very precise terms. And that is what **performance standards** (goals) *begin* to do. The next step in the process is to create **performance tasks.**

A performance task, also called an indicator, is a very precise opportunity to demonstrate that a student knows how to apply or use information. Having been taught multiplication, can Johnny figure out that if he sells three candy bars at $.50 his total is $.50 × 3? If Alexandra reads a paragraph on whales, can she figure out what the word *blubber* means from the context of the passage? These are the kinds of questions, sometimes called prompts, that evaluate whether or not a student has integrated learning for application in actual practice.

The tests that will measure your child's learning are being constructed around these very specific tasks. It is essential that you are familiar with the tasks that comprise your state's testing documents so that you can know exactly what your child should be learning and in what grade. You can then monitor his or her progress and support the process.

# Creating Tests to Measure Success

**B**efore we go any further, you should know that while H.R. 1, the *No Child Left Behind Act*, requires testing at grades three and eight to measure school improvement and achievement, this bill does *not* require federally sponsored national testing, nor does it establish national standards or federally controlled curriculum, or mandatory national teacher tests. Instead, the individual states construct their own testing programs, write their own curriculum, and establish their own guidelines for reporting to their constituents. Furthermore, local school districts use the state documents to develop their individual local curricula. But just as state report cards focus attention on local school districts, the national report card focuses attention on individual states. That is why it has become increasingly important for there to be some uniformity in standards from state to state.

Enter the national organizations such as the National Council of Teachers of Mathematics, the National Council of Teachers of English, the National Council for the Social Studies, the National Council of Science Teachers and so on. These national groups all have state groups, further broken down into regional groups, the purposes of which are to provide professional dialogue about current issues in the various content areas. These organizations provide seminars, training programs, conferences, and represent their members by establishing guidelines and recommendations for their practitioners. Therefore, even without a "federally required" curriculum in English, there is a national consensus, provided by the National Council, regarding content standards and assessment (testing) methods.

So it should not be surprising that given 50 states and 50 very different looking and sounding English, mathematics, social studies, and science curricula, there is incredible similarity! Let's examine English/Language Arts first.


## English/Language Arts

AFTER CAREFUL EXAMINATION of the English/Language Arts curriculum documents and test requirements in Texas, California, New York, Ohio, Pennsylvania, Florida, North Carolina, Georgia, Delaware, Maryland, Illinois, Connecticut, and New Jersey, remarkable consistency was found in the language used to describe the content standards for English/Language Arts.

For example:

New York students will be able to "Read, Write, Listen, and Speak for Information and Understanding, for Literary Response and Expression, for Critical Analysis and Evaluation, and for Social Interaction."

New Jersey students will "Speak for a variety of real purposes and audiences; listen actively in a variety of situations to inform from a variety of sources; write in clear, concise, organized language that varies in content and form for different audiences and purposes; read various materials and text with comprehension and critical analysis; view, understand, and use non-textual visual information."

Texas students will "Demonstrate a basic understanding of culturally diverse written texts; demonstrate an understanding of the effects of literary elements and techniques in culturally diverse written texts; demonstrate the ability to analyze and critically evaluate culturally diverse written texts and visual representations."

Florida students will "Construct meaning from informational text; construct meaning from literature."

North Carolina students will "Evaluate critically and analyze printed material and understand and apply accurately the rules of standard written English."

Maryland students will "Demonstrate the ability to respond to a text by employing personal experiences and critical analyses; compose in a variety of modes by developing content, employing specific forms, and selecting language appropriate for a particular audience and purpose; control language by applying the conventions of standard

English in writing and speaking; evaluate the content, organization, and language use of texts.

Connecticut students will "Read and respond to demonstrate basic understandings of text; read and respond to interpret or explain the text; explore and respond to classical and contemporary texts from many cultures and literary periods; read and respond to make judgments about the quality of the text."

California students will demonstrate "Word analysis, fluency, and systematic vocabulary development; reading comprehension with focus on informational material; literary response and analysis."

So it should not be surprising, then, that a list of performance standards, summarizing the content standards for reading and listening, might look like this:

1. Identify the main idea
2. Recognize supporting details
3. Draw inferences from text
4. Distinguish fact from opinion
5. Detect bias
6. Recognize propaganda
7. Recognize author's purpose
8. Identify logical relationships
9. Compare and contrast ideas
10. Read and interpret graphs, charts, and other visual text
11. Follow multi-step directions
12. Make predictions and draw conclusions
13. Recognize and interpret the use of literary elements in literature
14. Recognize and interpret the use of literary devices in literature
15. Define vocabulary from context
16. Recognize and apply the conventions of standard written English
17. Apply basic research skills to nonfiction
18. Listen for main idea, tone, purpose, detail, and fact
19. Interpret and use information from consumer and workplace documents
20. Apply personal experiences to both fiction and nonfiction

These 20 performance indicators vary from state to state in terms of emphasis, but they form the basis for developing those specific performance tasks, *by grade level*, that we talked about earlier. For example, there would likely never be a reading comprehension assessment that did not include a main idea question or a vocabulary in context question, but in grade three, the performance task (question) to measure main idea or vocabulary in context might be different. Additionally, some states might not emphasize detecting bias on an examination but it would certainly be part of classroom discussion.

Also important is the concept of *scaffolding* or *integrating* the various content standards. For instance, by the end of grade three, when most states give the first of their competency assessments in reading and math, the tests will measure skills taught and practiced in kindergarten, grade one, and grade two.

☛ **PARENT TIP:** As early as possible, ask your child to tell you the most important thing a story is trying to say. From a simple story, like *The Poky Little Puppy* (ages 3–6) to the more advanced *Fly Away Home* (ages 6 and up), paraphrasing "what the story is about" reinforces the concept of main idea.

Performance standards for writing and speaking in English/Language Arts might look something like this:

1. Establish focus by asserting a main or controlling idea.
2. Develop content using sufficient and appropriate supporting details.
3. Provide a logical pattern of organization with appropriate transitions and well-developed paragraphs.
4. Convey a sense of style with the use of varied and effective sentences, tone appropriate to the task and audience, and effective diction.
5. Control the conventions of standard written English including usage, mechanics, and sentence sense.

Again, the complexity of *main idea* on a grade three writing assessment won't look like the requirement for a *thesis statement* until the grade 11 assessment, but *main idea* is the writing concept that is introduced and reinforced up the grades so that by grade 11, students should be able to write a persuasive essay with a main idea established in the introductory paragraph.

Not every state tests writing the same way, but they are all looking for the same basic abilities, or performance standards, as itemized above. If you refer back to that fifth grade example in Chapter 1 and examine the evaluation, you will notice the references to style, control of conventions, and chronological order (organization). Whether it's fifth grade or second grade, the conventions of standard English and the concept of organization are important elements of written expression.

☛ **PARENT TIP:** By grade two and up, when your child has writing assignments to complete, set yourself up as the "reader" who asks questions. For
example, if you think a piece of writing is short and needs more details, ask,
"Can you tell me more?" or "Is there anything you can add to make this more
exciting?" This begins to develop a sense of audience—that writing is intended
to be read and understood by someone else. It also supports the idea that writing is important and worthy of discussion.

**PERFORMANCE TASKS**

Perhaps the most important part of the process of defining the standards and performance goals of any curriculum area is how it all translates into item types that children must respond to. What do you ask a third grader to do to measure his or her ability
to read effectively for main idea? The obvious answer is to present a block of text, have
it read, and then ask questions about it. In the past, traditional reading tests relied on
multiple-choice questions, with definite right or wrong answers.

While most English/Language Arts assessments still contain some multiple-choice
questions covering the skills (performance standards) listed above, today's tests go even
further. There is broad recognition that the only way to demonstrate whether a student
has read beyond mere surface comprehension is to require an *extended* response, a *constructed* response, or a *performance* response to the text. That means some form of writing. But whether it's reading, writing, listening, or speaking, one thing is clear—the task
requirements on today's tests demand much more of students. From longer passages,
to more complicated passages, to more writing, the bar has been raised. It is no longer
enough for a school system to write elaborate explanations of what they hope our children will be able to do. They now have to translate that rhetoric into specific skills and
tasks that our children must accomplish.

**THE NEW TESTS IN ENGLISH/LANGUAGE ARTS**

In the next chapters you will see actual test items with answer explanations and scoring guides for elementary, middle, and high school. But for right now, let's take a look
at the *what* and *why* of these tests.

First, the day of the all multiple-choice test is gone. If your state hasn't already
rewritten its English/Language Arts assessments, it will. Whether it requires separate
reading and writing tests, or a test that combines both, your child will have to demonstrate writing skills. The new H.R. 1 bill targets reading and math testing, but few reading tests today isolate reading from writing, listening, and speaking.

Most English/Language Arts exams integrate the communication strands (reading, writing, listening, and speaking). That is, students may be asked to read and write a response as part of a reading comprehension test. They also could be given a stand-alone writing prompt which is designed to measure technical writing skill totally separate from reading comprehension. Or both! A writing test that asks for a response to a piece of reading is called a *text-based* response. A writing assignment with no text to read is called a *stand-alone* response. In either case, the ability to put pen to paper and write is critical. In addition to the parent tip, another important thing for you to consider is how much writing your child is being asked to do in school. Is the teacher incorporating short writing assignments into his or her daily class work? Do your child's tests require writing in addition to short answer questions? Whether it is third grade or eleventh grade, whether it's English or social studies, if all your child has are short answer tests, it's time for a conference with the teacher. Remember, it's not only in English that the tests are changing. When we look at the math, social studies, and science exams, you will see that writing is an essential method of evaluation.

Most English/Language Arts assessments combine fiction and nonfiction passages to which children must respond. The ability to read the newspaper and to analyze and interpret advertising, graphs, charts, and historical documents is a vital skill for citizens of a participatory democracy. Hence, *document literacy* is a new emphasis. In California, for instance, the ability to read consumer documents such as bus schedules, leases, and warranties feature prominently on their high school exit exam in English/Language Arts. In New York, Ohio, Pennsylvania, and North Carolina, consumer documents and nonfiction pieces that include graphs, charts, and tables are used. Another new term is *authentic* materials, meaning that they come from the texts of daily experience like the daily newspaper. English no longer means just literature.

Another new feature of the English/Language Arts assessments is *text integrity*. There used to be many short passages, often excerpts from longer pieces, which formed the basis of the questions. Today, whole short stories, essays, articles, and editorials, even the text of speeches, form the basis of reading comprehension questions. Thus, children have to read longer, more complex text than ever before. You can help by encouraging your child to read newspaper and magazine articles. You can also help your child develop the ability to read more effectively by asking questions about the details of his or her efforts.

☛ **PARENT TIP:**
- Encourage your child to read the newspaper every day.
- Discuss an editorial every day and identify the main point of the writer.
- Subscribe to a quality children's magazine or news magazine for older children.
- Provide practice reading!

Yet another feature of the newer English/Language Arts assessments is the inclusion of a listening comprehension question. Not all states require this type of question; New York and New Jersey do—to name just two. Find out if your state has such a question and practice listening strategies with your child. After listening to the evening news, ask your child to paraphrase what he or she heard. Ask him or her to recall details.

In some states (New Jersey, for example), children are asked to look at a picture and create a narrative of personal experience as part of the writing test. This leads to a word about writing tests.

### WRITING

There are three main purposes for writing: to inform, to persuade, and to narrate. Many states build these purposes into a whole English/Language Arts (ELA) test, but some still have separate experiences. And it also depends on the level. Elementary ELA tests are different from middle school tests, and middle school tests are different from the high school graduation requirement exams. New York, for instance, has replaced its high school graduation requirement—Competency Test in Writing—with the comprehensive English/Language Arts Regents Examination that builds writing into the exam requirements for responding to documents and literary text. But Ohio, Connecticut, Pennsylvania, and Delaware, to name just a few states, have separate writing tests that require passing grades for a high school diploma. Pennsylvania requires three writing tasks. California requires two. Variations continue throughout the 50 states. If you want to know exactly how your state evaluates writing, you must visit its website or request a conference with your child's principal or district office curriculum director. Remember, the more you know, the better able you will be to anticipate and support your child's development.

☞ **PARENT TIP:** Every writing program, at every grade level, practices narrating (telling a story) from personal experience. Use a family photograph and ask your child to "tell the story of the time" this picture was taken. Probe for details of time, place, and people.

## <u>Mathematics</u>

JUST AS THERE was remarkable consistency in the language used to describe the content standards for English/Language Arts, there is similar congruity in the content standards for mathematics from state to state.

For example:

New York students will communicate and reason mathematically by:

- ▶ applying mathematics in real-world settings.
- ▶ solving problems through the integrated study of number systems, geometry, algebra, data analysis, probability, and trigonometry.

California students will:

- ▶ develop fluency in basic computational skills.
- ▶ develop an understanding of mathematical concepts.
- ▶ become mathematical problem solvers who can recognize and solve routine problems readily and find ways to reach a solution or goal where no routine path is apparent.
- ▶ communicate precisely about quantities, logical relationships, and unknown values through the use of signs, symbols, models, graphs, and mathematical terms.
- ▶ reason mathematically by gathering data, analyzing evidence, and building arguments to support or refute hypotheses.
- ▶ make connections among mathematical ideas and between mathematics and other disciplines.

New Jersey students will:

- ▶ develop the ability to pose and solve mathematical problems in mathematics, other disciplines, and everyday experiences.

- ▶ communicate mathematically through written, oral, symbolic, and visual forms of expression.

- ▶ connect mathematics to other learning by understanding the inter-relationships of mathematical ideas and the roles that mathematics and mathematical modeling play in other disciplines and in life.

- ▶ develop reasoning ability and become self-reliant, independent mathematical thinkers.

- ▶ regularly and routinely use calculators, computers, manipulatives, and other mathematical tools to enhance mathematical thinking, understanding, and power.

- ▶ develop number sense and an ability to represent numbers in a variety of forms and use numbers in diverse situations.

- ▶ develop spatial sense and an ability to use geometric properties and relationships to solve problems in mathematics and everyday life.

- ▶ understand, select, and apply various methods of performing numerical operations.

- ▶ develop an understanding of and use measurement to describe and analyze phenomena.

- ▶ use a variety of estimation strategies and recognize situations in which estimation is appropriate.

- ▶ develop an understanding of patterns, relationships, and functions and use them to represent and explain real-world phenomena.

- ▶ develop an understanding of statistics and probability and use them to describe sets of data, model situations, and support appropriate inferences and arguments.

- ▶ develop an understanding of algebraic concepts and processes and use them to represent and analyze relationships among variable quantities and to solve problems.

- ▶ apply the concepts and methods of discrete mathematics to model and explore a variety of practical situations.

- ▶ develop an understanding of the conceptual building blocks of calculus and use them to model and analyze natural phenomena.

- ▶ demonstrate high levels of mathematical thought through experiences which extend beyond traditional computation, algebra, and geometry.

Louisiana students will:

- ▶ in problem solving investigations, demonstrate an understanding of the real number system and communicate the relationships within that system using a variety of techniques and tools.
- ▶ in problem solving investigations, demonstrate an understanding of concepts and processes that allow them to analyze, represent, and describe relationships among variable quantities and to apply algebraic methods to real-world situations.
- ▶ in problem solving investigations, demonstrate an understanding of the concepts, processes, and real-life applications of measurement.
- ▶ in problem solving investigations, demonstrate an understanding of geometric concepts and applications involving one-, two-, and three-dimensional geometry, and justify their findings.
- ▶ in problem solving investigations, discover trends, formulate conjectures regarding cause and effect relationships, and demonstrate critical thinking skills in order to make informed decisions.
- ▶ in problem solving investigations, demonstrate an understanding of patterns, relationships, and functions that represent and explain real-world situations.

Alaska students will:

- ▶ understand mathematical facts, concepts, principles, and theories.
- ▶ understand and be able to select and use a variety of problem solving strategies.
- ▶ understand and be able to form and use appropriate methods to define and explain mathematical relationships.
- ▶ use logic and reason to solve mathematical problems.
- ▶ apply mathematical concepts and processes to situations within and outside of school.

Arizona students will:

- ▶ develop number sense and use numbers and number relationships to acquire basic facts, to solve a wide variety of real-world problems, and to determine the reasonableness of results.
- ▶ use data collection and analysis, statistics, and probability to make valid inferences, decisions, and arguments and to solve a variety of real-world problems.
- ▶ use algebraic methods to explore, model, and describe pattern, relationships and functions involving numbers, shapes, data, and graphs within a variety of real-world problem solving situations.

▶ use geometric methods, properties, and relationships as a means to recognize, draw, describe, connect, and analyze shapes and representations in the physical world.

▶ make and use direct and indirect measurement—metric and U.S. customary—to describe and compare the real world and to prepare for the study of discrete functions, fractals, and chaos that have evolved out of the age of technology.

▶ use both inductive and deductive reasoning as they make conjectures and test the validity of arguments.

In mathematics, the emphasis is on problem solving, investigating, and real-life and real-world applications of concepts. Summarizing the content standards, the following content strands emerge as basics for mathematics instruction in all states:

1. Number Sense
2. Data Analysis and Probability
3. Patterns, Algebra, and Functions
4. Geometry
5. Measurement and Discrete Mathematics
6. Mathematical Structure/Logic

Under each of these strands the various states enumerate a variety of performance standards, by grade level, specific to each strand. There are many performance standards that can be listed under each strand and some states are very detailed and specific. A very general summary looks like this:

1. Represent and use real numbers in a variety of equivalent forms.
2. Solve problems involving numeric equations or inequalities.
3. Estimate and compute with real numbers.
4. Use computational methods as problem-solving tools.
5. Construct, draw, measure, estimate.
6. Collect, organize, analyze, and interpret data.
7. Perform basic arithmetic functions.
8. Use inductive and deductive reasoning to formulate and test arguments.
9. Read and interpret graphs, charts, and tables.
10. Make predictions.
11. Describe and compare the attributes of plane and solid geometric figures.

As was the case with English/Language Arts, these mathematics performance standards form the basis for the development of specific performance tasks to measure a student's accomplishment.



As was true in English/Language Arts, the new math tests will not always be strictly multiple choice. Although mathematics questions certainly require correct answers, the new math tests want to see more than just an answer; they want to see how the answer was derived. That means that some questions may require that a student show his or her calculations and his or her methods for arriving at an answer.

For example, one of the performance tasks in New York for grade eight reads as follows:

> I. Develop and apply the Pythagorean principle in the solution of problems.

This performance task translates into a question such as:

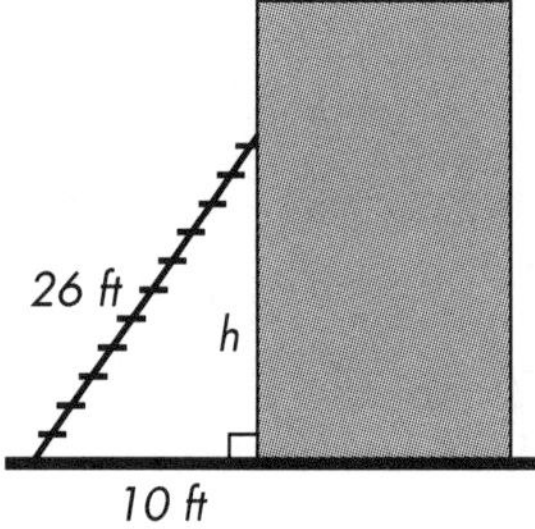


> The base of a ladder rests on the ground ten feet from the edge of the building, as shown above. Use the information presented in the diagram to calculate the height, $h$, from the ground to the point where the top of the ladder touches the building.

> Show your work.

Answer:

Notice how this question requires that the student record his or her calculations as he or she works in a step by step fashion to arrive upon an answer. For full credit, a student would indicate the following:

$$a^2 + b^2 = c^2$$
$$10^2 + b^2 = 26^2$$
$$100 + b^2 = 676$$
$$\underline{-100 \qquad -100}$$
$$b^2 = 576$$
$$b = 24 \text{ ft}$$

Students may receive partial credit for answers that followed a logical process but contained a miscalculation along the way.

Note that some students have the capacity to spot 3-4-5 and 5-12-13 right triangles. Here, a shrewd eighth grader may have noticed that this triangle is just a double of a 5-12-13 triangle, namely 10-24-26. However, this student should write down:

> This triangle is in proportion with a 5-12-13 right triangle and would therefore be similar to a 5-12-13 right triangle. Each side of this triangle is double the length of the corresponding sides of the 5-12-13 triangle. Thus, the missing side would be $12 \times 2 = 24$ ft.

In this case, simply spotting the Pythagorean triplet and writing "24 feet" may have cost your child a point on the test. It is important to show calculations and to describe the thought process that led to the answer.

You may also have noticed the reiteration of phrases like *problem solving investigations, real-world problems, real-life applications, and real-world settings.* This means that on any given mathematics test, the questions are likely to be put in the context of a real life application. For example,

> In California, one performance task under Measure and Geometry reads as follows:
>
> 1.0 Students choose and use appropriate units and measurement tools to quantify the property of objects.

This performance task translates into a question such as:

Amy needs to measure the length of the paintbrush above. What unit below would be the <u>best</u> unit for her to use?

**a.** grams

**b.** meters

**c.** cups

**d.** inches

Notice how this question requires the third grader to visualize the size of a real-world object and to comprehend the sizes and functions of metric and U.S. units in order to assess which one would be appropriate. Here, a child will look at choice **a** and recognize that grams measure *weight* (actually *mass*). Choice **b,** meters, is a unit used to measure length, but the child must keep in mind that she wants the "best" unit. *Meters may not be the best unit.* The child next addresses choice **c,** cups, and deems this choice inappropriate. Whereas an adult may be cognizant that cups measure *capacity*, a successful third grader will pass up choice **c** with a mental image of a "cup of water" and will laughingly eliminate this choice with this notion in mind. If your child makes it to choice **d** (the correct answer), and chooses it over **b,** then he or she has demonstrated that he or she has the ability to choose appropriate units of measurement.

The high school exit exam in mathematics in New York (New York State Regents Math A) requires 15 performance task items as well as 20 multiple-choice questions, and all questions will "require applications to real-world situations."

In Ohio, the high school graduation exam will use 44 multiple-choice, four short answer, and two extended response questions. All will be "drawn from real-world contexts."

In Maryland, the high school exit exam will require "Single response, brief constructed response, and extended constructed response items which will require students to solve real-world problems with graphic representation playing an important role."

In Connecticut there will be 24 multiple-choice and eight open-ended questions from "real-world scenarios" on the high school exam.

In New Jersey there will be 26–31 multiple-choice items, seven open-ended items, and four short constructed response items on the high school exam.

The list could go on. Every state is moving to the same format, although multiple-choice questions remain a mainstay of most content area exams.

Another important feature of the mathematics exams is the permitted use of calculators; some states even permit the use of graphing calculators and/or scientific calculators. Some states go so far as to provide a "reference sheet" of geometry formulas to assist students. Students are being encouraged to use the technology available to them.

> ☞ **PARENT TIP:** Using the nutrition guide on a loaf of bread, ask your child to calculate how many calories would be in a double portion. Repeat this for double or triple servings of any product. Not only is this mathematics at work, it's an opportunity to pay attention to nutrition!

A word about social studies and science: Though not part of H.R. 1 *No Child Left Behind,* social studies and science are also being tested in in elementary, middle, and high school. Many states require that students demonstrate competency in these areas in order to earn a high school diploma. Like the ELA and mathematics tests, social studies and science exams are requiring more writing to answer performance-based questions.

So whether it's English/Language Arts or mathematics, social studies or science, the content standards are being defined, the performance standards are being established by grade, and the performance tasks are being set, all leading to tests which will determine whether your child is meeting the demands of a new, more rigorous program of study. These new performance tests in English/Language Arts and mathematics, offered in grades 3–8, are designed to provide YOU, the parent, with the information you need to know to find out how well your child is doing in school. Perhaps most important, you'll find out how well the school is doing in educating your child. By the time your child reaches high school and takes the exit exams, there should be no surprises. The stakes are very high when a student can go through 12 years of school and fail to meet exit requirements to earn a high school diploma. It is imperative that you and your child know how to prepare by understanding what is required.

Now let's look at examples of the kinds of questions which will be used on the tests in English/Language Arts and mathematics.

# Looking at High School Exit Exams: English/Language Arts

**Even before** the passage of the *No Child Left Behind Act,* most states required that students be tested at least once in English/Language Arts in elementary school sometime between grades three through five, in middle or junior high school between grades six through nine, and in high school between grades 10–12. Many states had basic competency requirements in reading, writing, and mathematics as exit requirements—a requirement for a high school diploma. Most elementary testing occurred, and still does occur, in grade four, with some states opting for a separate writing assessment in grade five.

In addition to providing important information about a school's performance, a primary purpose of elementary school testing is to identify students who might be having difficulty accomplishing grade level expectations and who, therefore, might be in danger of not performing well on the state exit exam. The goal was and still is to get help as soon as possible to those students who seem in danger of not earning a high school diploma.

Many states have requirements in place for any child who falls below a certain reference point to receive specific remedial services ranging from regularly scheduled extra classes in reading to special after-school tutorials. The premise is that if you can intervene early enough, then no child should reach high school unable to satisfy the exit exam requirements and be "left behind" without a high school diploma.

To be sure that this intervention works, another round of testing occurs in middle or junior high school, usually in grade eight. Once again, the primary purpose of this testing is to provide an additional safety net for children who are not meeting grade level expectations and are therefore deemed in danger of not meeting the high school graduation requirements. No child or parent wants to find out in the tenth or eleventh grade that after ten, eleven, even twelve years of school, a high school diploma is out of reach.

So let's take a look at what some high school exit exams in English/Language Arts look like. Remember, there is similarity among the states, but to see exactly what your state and your school district specifically require, you should go to the state education department website or visit your building principal. A complete list of state websites is presented in Appendix A.

## High School Exit Exams: At Stake Is a High School Diploma

REMEMBER THE FOUR language arts strands? They are reading, writing, listening, and speaking. Just what determines and then measures a high school student's competency in these four areas?

First, we must take a look at how testing is tied to course requirements. Your school district may still use ability placement as the basis for choosing which courses your child will take. You know, the "easier" English class or the "not college-bound" class. However, most research indicates that segregating students by ability simply reduces expectations and hence performance, so the current movement in education is to eliminate ability groupings and require one standard for all—a high standard!

However, as the phasing out of ability-designated classes proceeds, most states still have English/Language Arts competency tests in place to serve those students who do not take the end-of-course English exams that will satisfy the graduation standards. For example, in New York State, as of June 2002, all students must pass the New York State Comprehensive Regents Examination in English in order to earn a high school diploma. There will no longer be the easier Basic Competency Test in Reading and Writing. But in Texas, the Texas Assessment of Knowledge and Skills (TAKS) *or* an end of course English examination are both ways to satisfy the testing requirement. The difference is that a student who chooses a less challenging class must still pass a more rigorous examination because the TAKS test is not just an "easy" test for kids who took less challenging classes. It may not be tied to a specific course in English literature, but it is a demanding reading/writing exam.

The rigor of the exam is determined by the demands of the test and testing in English/Language Arts takes time—lots of it. Gone are the days of the two-hour final or minimum competency test. Most state exams in ELA require two days of three or more hours of test time whether it's the state designated test, such as Texas' TAKS, or an end-of-course test.

## What They All Have in Common

MOST HIGH SCHOOL English/Language Arts assessments require a combination of reading and writing for the purposes of narration, persuasion, and exposition. Often, reading comprehension is measured with a series of traditional multiple-choice questions followed by open-ended or performance based questions that require an elaborated written response. But one thing all the tests have in common is that the reading or listening passages are longer and more challenging than ever before.

Let's take a look at a sample reading/writing question—based on a narrative (short story)—that could appear on a high school exit exam. First, it is the full text of a short story, rather than an excerpt. This means longer sustained, silent reading; it requires that a student remember more details. The questions that follow expect a student to be able to identify tone, mood, and attitude. And the open-ended responses require more thoughtful reading that also goes beyond surface, literal comprehension of stated details into interpretation and analysis. The open-ended writing questions are not designed to measure writing competency per se, but do provide a more in-depth look at reading ability beyond surface comprehension.

Students would be expected to read the following short story and respond to the questions that follow.

## Miss Brill
### by Katherine Mansfield

Although it was so brilliantly fine—the blue sky powdered with gold and the great spots of light like white wine splashed over the Jardins Publiques*—Miss Brill was glad that she had decided on her fur[†]. The air was motionless, but when you opened your mouth there was just a faint chill, like a chill from a glass of iced water before you sip, and now and again a leaf came drifting—from nowhere, from the sky. Miss Brill put up her hand and touched her fur. Dear little thing! It was nice to feel it again. She had taken it out of its box that afternoon, shaken out the moth-powder, given it a good brush, and rubbed the life back into the dim little eyes. "What has been happening to me?" said the sad little eyes. Oh, how sweet it was to see them snap at her again from the red eiderdown!. . . . But the nose, which was of some black composition, wasn't at all firm. It must have had a knock, somehow. Never mind—a little dab of black sealing-wax when the time came—when it was absolutely necessary. . . . Little rogue! Yes, she really felt like that about it. Little rogue biting its tail just by her left ear. She could have taken it off and laid it on her lap and stroked it. She felt a tingling in her hands and arms, but that came from walking, she supposed. And when she breathed, something light and sad—no, not sad, exactly—something gentle seemed to move in her bosom.

There were a number of people out this afternoon, far more than last Sunday. And the band sounded louder and gayer. That was because the Season had begun. For although the band played all the year round on Sundays, out of season it was never the same. It was like someone playing with only the family to listen; it didn't care how it played if there weren't any strangers present. Wasn't the conductor wearing a new coat, too? She was sure it was new. He scraped with his foot and flapped his arms like a rooster about to crow, and the bandsmen sitting in the green rotunda blew out their cheeks and glared at the music. Now there came a little "flutey" bit—very pretty!—a little chain of bright drops. She was sure it would be repeated. It was; she lifted her head and smiled.

Only two people shared her "special" seat: a fine old man in a velvet coat, his hands clasped over a huge carved walking-stick, and a big old woman, sitting upright, with a roll of knitting on her embroidered apron. They did not speak. This was disappointing, for Miss Brill always looked forward to the conversation. She had become really quite expert, she thought, at listening as though she didn't listen, at sitting in other people's lives just for a minute while they talked round her.

She glanced, sideways, at the old couple. Perhaps they would go soon. Last Sunday, too, hadn't been as interesting as usual. An Englishman and his wife, he wearing a dreadful Panama hat and she button boots. And she'd gone on the whole time about how she ought to wear spectacles; she knew she needed them; but that it was no good getting any; they'd be sure to break and they'd never keep on. And he'd been so patient. He'd suggested everything—gold rims, the kind that curved round your ears, little pads inside the bridge. No, nothing would please her. "They'll always be sliding down my nose!" Miss Brill had wanted to shake her.

The old people sat on the bench, still as statues. Never mind, there was always the crowd to watch. To and fro, in front of the flower-beds and the band rotunda, the couples and groups paraded, stopped to talk, to greet, to buy a handful of flowers from the old beggar who had his tray fixed to the railings. Little children ran among them, swooping and laughing; little boys with big white silk bows under their chins; little girls, little French dolls, dressed up in velvet and lace. And sometimes a tiny staggerer came suddenly rocking into the open from under the trees, stopped, stared, as suddenly sat down "flop" until its small high-stepping mother, like a young hen, rushed scolding to its rescue. Other people sat on the benches and green chairs, but they were nearly always the same, Sunday after Sunday, and—Miss Brill had often noticed—there was something funny about nearly all of them. They were odd, silent, nearly all old, and from the way they stared they looked as though they'd just come from dark little rooms or even—even cupboards!

Behind the rotunda the slender trees with yellow leaves down drooping, and through them just a line of sea, and beyond the blue sky with gold-veined clouds.

Tum-tum-tum tiddle-um! tiddle-um! tum tiddley-um tum ta! blew the band.

Two young girls in red came by and two young soldiers in blue met them, and they laughed and paired and went off arm in arm. Two peasant women with funny straw hats passed, gravely, leading beautiful smoke-coloured donkeys. A cold, pale nun hurried by. A beautiful woman came along and dropped her bunch of violets, and a little boy ran after to hand them to her, and she took them and threw them away as if they'd been poisoned. Dear me! Miss Brill didn't know whether to admire that or not! And now an ermine toque‡ and a gentleman in grey met just in front of her. He was tall, stiff, dignified, and she was wearing the ermine toque she'd bought when her hair was yellow. Now everything, her hair, her face, even her eyes, was the same colour as the shabby ermine, and her hand, in its cleaned glove, lifted to dab her lips, was a tiny yellowish paw. Oh, she was so pleased to see him—delighted! She rather thought they were going to meet that afternoon. She described where she'd been—everything, here, there, along the sea. The day was so charming—didn't he agree? And wouldn't he, perhaps? . . . But he shook his head, lighted a cigarette, slowly breathed a great deep puff into her face and, even while she was still talking and laughing, flicked the match away and walked on. The ermine toque was alone; she smiled more brightly than ever. But even the band seemed to know what she was feeling and played more sloftly, played tenderly, and the drum beat "The Brute! The Brute!" over and over. What would she do? What was going to happen now? But as Miss Brill wondered, the ermine toque turned, raised her hand as though she'd seen someone else, much nicer, just over there, and pattered away. And the band changed again and played more quickly, more gaily than ever, and the old couple on Miss Brill's seat got up and marched away, and such a funny old man with long whiskers hobbled along in time to the music and was nearly knocked over by four girls walking abreast.

Oh, how fascinating it was! How she enjoyed it! How she loved sitting here, watching it all! It was like a play. It was exactly like a play. Who could believe the sky at the back wasn't painted? But it wasn't till a little brown dog trotted on solemnly and then slowly trotted off, like a little "theatre" dog, a little dog that had been drugged, that Miss Brill discovered what it was that made it so exciting. They were all on the stage. They weren't only the audience, not only looking on; they were acting. Even she had a part and came every Sunday. No doubt somebody would have noticed if she hadn't been there; she was part of the performance, after all. How strange she'd never thought of it like that before! And yet it explained why she made such a point of starting from home at just the same time each week—so as not to be late for the performance—and it also explained why

  A Parent's Guide to High Stakes Testing

she had quite a queer, shy feeling at telling her English pupils how she spent her Sunday afternoons. No wonder! Miss Brill nearly laughed out loud. She was on the stage. She thought of the old invalid gentleman to whom she read the newspaper four afternoons a week while he slept in the garden. She had got quite used to the frail head on the cotton pillow, the hollowed eyes, the open mouth and the high pinched nose. If he'd been dead she mightn't have noticed for weeks; she wouldn't have minded. But suddenly he knew he was having the paper read to him by an actress! "An actress!" The old head lifted; two points of light quivered in the old eyes. "An actress—are ye?" And Miss Brill smoothed the newspaper as though it were the manuscript of her part and said gently: "Yes, I have been an actress for a long time."

The band had been having a rest. Now they started again. And what they played was warm, sunny, yet there was just a faint chill—a something, what was it?—not sadness—no, not sadness—a something that made you want to sing. The tune lifted, lifted, the light shone; and it seemed to Miss Brill that in another moment all of them, all the whole company, would begin singing. The young ones, the laughing ones who were moving together, they would begin, and the men's voices, very resolute and brave, would join them. And then she too, she too, and the others on the benches—they would come in with a kind of accompaniment—something low, that scarcely rose or fell, something so beautiful—moving. . . . And Miss Brill's eyes filled with tears and she looked smiling at all the other members of the company. Yes, we understand, we understand, she thought—though what they understood she didn't know.

Just at that moment a boy and a girl came and sat down where the old couple had been. They were beautifully dressed; they were in love. The hero and heroine, of course, just arrived from his father's yacht. And still soundlessly singing, still with that trembling smile, Miss Brill prepared to listen.

"No, not now," said the girl. "Not here, I can't."

"But why? Because of that stupid old thing at the end there?" asked the boy. "Why does she come here at all—who wants her? Why doesn't she keep her silly old mug at home?"

"It's her fu-fur which is so funny," giggled the girl. "It's exactly like a fried whiting."

"Ah, be off with you!" said the boy in an angry whisper. Then: "Tell me, ma petite chérie—"

"No, no here," said the girl. "Not *yet.*"

On her way home she usually bought a slice of honey-cake at the baker's. It was her Sunday treat. Sometimes there was an almond in her slice, sometimes not. It made a great difference. If there was an almond it was like carrying home a tiny present—a surprise—something that might very well not have been there. She hurried on the almond Sundays and struck the match for the kettle in quite a dashing way. But today she passed the baker's by, climbed the stairs, went into the little dark room—her room like a cupboard—and sat down on the red eiderdown. She sat there for a long time. The box that the fur came out of was on the bed. She unclasped the necklet quickly; quickly, without looking, laid it inside. But when she put the lid on she thought she heard something crying.

### *Vocabulary:*

*Jardins Publiques are public gardens or a park.

†The "fur" refers to the fur scarf that Miss Brill wears. It is made of the skin of a small animal with its legs, feet, and head still attached.

‡The "ermine toque" referred to is a close fitting hat made from the white fur of an ermine, a small animal related to the weasel. In this paragraph Miss Brill refers to the woman who is wearing the ermine toque by calling her an "ermine toque."


Before we look at the questions that follow, it is important to know that there are two levels of reading comprehension questions: literal and inferential (interpretive). The answers to the former questions can be found explicitly stated in the text. They tend to be questions of who, when, and where. The latter set of questions, however, probe beyond the surface and reach to why and how. A reader must be able to interpret information to answer. Reading comprehension questions that rely solely on literal questions are very rare in the new assessments!

First, let's look at the multiple-choice questions that follow. See if you can identify which are literal and which are inferential. A complete set of answer/explanations follows the questions.


## MULTIPLE-CHOICE QUESTIONS

1. According to the story, Miss Brill enjoys going to the park because
    a. she loves the music in the park.
    b. she loves showing off her furs.
    c. she loves watching the dramas acted out by the people around her.
    d. she has nothing better to do with her time.

2. What does the young couple who sits on the bench next to Miss Brill do?
   a. They argue.
   b. They make fun of Miss Brill.
   c. They kiss.
   d. They ask Miss Brill for advice.

3. The boy's angry "Ah, be off with you!" in paragraph 15 is directed to
   a. Miss Brill.
   b. the girl.
   c. a bird.
   d. the old man whose seat they'd taken.

4. Who or what is making the crying noise Miss Brill thinks she hears at the end of the story?
   a. the fur
   b. Miss Brill
   c. Miss Brill's neighbor
   d. the girl who was sitting on the bench next to Miss Brill.

5. Miss Brill's affection for her fur suggests that
   a. she feels sorry for animals killed for fur.
   b. someone special had given her the fur.
   c. she is grateful for the warmth it provides.
   d. the fur reminds her of a time when she was happier.

6. A significant portion of the story is devoted to describing the people in the park. The narrator does this in order to show
   a. that the story takes place in a French, not American, town.
   b. what kind of people were in the park.
   c. how much Miss Brill enjoys watching people in the park.
   d. that Miss Brill has a photographic memory.

7. At the end of the story, Miss Brill has realized that
   a. she is just as "odd" as the others she sees in the park every Sunday.
   b. she needs a new fur.
   c. she is too critical of others.
   d. she does not belong in the park anymore.

8. Several times in the story, Miss Brill feels "a faint chill" in the air, something sad but "not sad, exactly" (paragraphs one and ten). The author repeats this detail in order to
   a. help readers clearly imagine the weather.
   b. suggest that Miss Brill is dying.
   c. balance the otherwise happy tone of the story.
   d. foreshadow the ending of the story.

9. The story tells us that Miss Brill "had become really quite expert, she thought, at listening as though she didn't listen, at sitting in on other people's lives just for a minute while they talked around her" (paragraph three). This suggests that
   a. Miss Brill is lonely and doesn't have many people to talk to.
   b. Miss Brill is nosy and likes to get involved in other people's business.
   c. Miss Brill is a very good listener.
   d. Miss Brill is terribly shy and is afraid to talk to others.

10. In the center of the story, Miss Brill realizes that "[t]hey were all on the stage" in the park. How does this realization make her feel?
   a. afraid of being judged as she judges others
   b. happy to be part of the action, not just the audience
   c. nervous about telling the blind man that she's actually an actress
   d. ashamed of how small her role is

**ANSWERS AND EXPLANATIONS—MULTIPLE-CHOICE QUESTIONS**

1. **c.** This is a literal question. This answer is clearly stated in paragraph nine, which states, "Oh, how fascinating it was! How she enjoyed it! How she loved sitting here, watching it all! It was like a play." In addition, paragraph eight focuses on a small drama being acted out by the "ermine toque" and the gentleman she meets. Further, the amount of time devoted to describing the various people in the park is additional evidence that Miss Brill goes to the park to watch people. She does love the music in the park (**a**), but this is not the main reason she goes. She may be proud of her fur (**b**) and she may not have much else to do on a Sunday (**d**), but there isn't evidence in the story to support either of these answers.

2. **b.** This is an interpretive question. The story doesn't say they make fun of her but it is clear that they do. The boy calls her a "stupid old thing" and wonders why she doesn't "keep her silly old mug at home" (paragraph 13). The girl states,

"It's her fu-fur which is so funny" (paragraph 14). The boy does speak angrily in paragraph 15, but the angry comment is directed towards Miss Brill.

3. **a.** This is an interpretive question. The answer lies in the description, " . . . in an angry whisper." These words are addressed to Miss Brill. This inference can be drawn from the shift in tone. The boy has been speaking earnestly and lovingly to the girl, but these words are spoken angrily. Further, the boy believes that the girl won't do what he wants (which is to kiss him) because "of that stupid old thing at the end there"—and they have just sat down on Miss Brill's bench.

4. **b.** This is an interpretive question. Though it isn't directly stated in the story, we can infer that Miss Brill lives alone in her "little dark room" (paragraph 18). That her name is *Miss* Brill indicates that she was never married, and because her room is small, it's unlikely that she shares it with a roommate. Besides, there's no mention of anyone else in her life except the old man to whom she reads the newspaper and her students. Thus, it's logical to infer that she lives alone, and therefore the only person who could be crying is she. The fur, of course, is dead and cannot cry (**a**), though she imagines so. We know she is in her room, so it cannot be the girl from the park (**d**), and though it's possible that she might have heard her neighbor crying through the walls (**c**), the fact that Miss Brill didn't get her usual honey cake suggests that she is very upset, and it's logical to conclude that she is upset enough to cry.

5. **d.** This is an interpretive question. Though Miss Brill takes out the fur because there's a "faint chill" in the air, she is not fond of her fur because it is warm (**c**) but because it reminds her of a time when she was younger and happier. This is suggested by the fact that the fur is old (it is covered in moth-powder, needs brushing and needs "the life" rubbed "back into the dim little eyes") and by how good she feels when she touches it. She calls it a "dear little thing" and "little rogue" two times, which suggests that she may have been a bit of a little rogue herself when she was younger and the fur wasn't so old. It is possible that the fur was given to her by someone special (**b**), but there is no evidence for this in the story, nor is there evidence that she feels sorry for animals killed for fur.

6. **c.** This is an interpretive question. The description is designed to reflect how much Miss Brill enjoys watching people in the park. Though the story is told by a third person, limited omniscient narrator, what the narrator describes is what we might see from Miss Brill's point of view. We are able to see the people whom she is watching. The story could just as easily take place in an American seaside town as a French one (**a**), so the country is not important, and there's no evidence that Miss Brill has a photographic memory (**d**). True, the description gives us a

sense of the kind of people who are in the park (**b**), but the main goal of the description is to show us what Miss Brill sees and how much she enjoys watching others.

7. **a.** This is an interpretive question. When the boy and girl make fun of her—and especially her fur—Miss Brill realizes that she is just as odd as the other people she sees in the park every Sunday. In paragraph 5, Miss Brill describes the other "regulars"—the people who were there "Sunday after Sunday"—and notes that "there was something funny about nearly all of them. They were odd, silent, nearly all old, and from the way they stared they looked as though they'd just come from dark little rooms or even—even cupboards!" At the end of the story, after Miss Brill has realized that she is one of those funny old people, the narrator describes her room as a "little dark room—her room like a cupboard." She sees that she is just like them.

8. **d.** This is an interpretive question. Miss Brill is cheerful and the day is beautiful, but beneath the cheer there is a sadness, a longing, and this feeling is reflected in the weather—it's beautiful but there's something not quite right in the air, something that Miss Brill wants to call sadness but does not. She wants to fight off the sadness, to pretend it isn't there, and symbolically she puts on the fur to protect herself. But the fur is from her past, and instead of fending off the sadness, it brings it on, in the end, by leading her to be mocked by the young couple. There is no evidence that Miss Brill is ill or otherwise at death's door (**b**), and at any rate the focus of the story isn't her physical health but her emotional well being. Though there are numerous exclamation points and happy, affectionate phrases throughout the story (**c**), the sad undercurrent is evident from the beginning (the story even begins with "although"). Finally, there is some detailed description of the weather (**a**), but the description of the chill in the air serves a much more important purpose.

9. **a.** This is an interpretive question. Miss Brill is lonely. She is not nosy (**b**) because she doesn't speculate about the "characters" she watches; she doesn't wonder, for example, what sort of relationship the "ermine toque" had with the gentleman, and she certainly doesn't talk to others and ask personal questions. She may be shy (**d**), but since she is an English teacher (paragraph nine), she probably isn't so shy that she's frightened to talk to others. Miss Brill may be a good listener (**c**), but the fact that she spends the whole time in the park listening instead of talking with others suggests that she doesn't have anyone in her life to whom she can talk regularly and intimately. She comes to the park alone and goes home alone. She listens to others to live vicariously through them for a short while.

**10.** **b.** This is an interpretive question. Miss Brill had thought of herself as an audience member, as someone who only watched what was happening "on stage." When she realizes that she's on the stage, too, she is very excited. Perhaps someone is also watching *her*—and it's exciting to think that she's interesting enough to be watched and that she might take part in the action. There is no evidence that she's afraid of being judged (**a**) or that she's ashamed of her small role (**d**)— on the contrary, she's glad to have a part. Further, paragraph nine shows that she's clearly excited about telling the old man (**c**); she imagines the conversation that would take place next time she sees him.

Notice that only one of the ten questions is literal. That means that the answer is stated directly in the text. All the other questions rely on the reader's ability to use details to infer attitude, tone, mood, or purpose. Inferring, interpreting, and analyzing are the key strategies that must be used.

Three of the choices given (**a–d**) are called "distractors." They are commonly written to include the following four types of incorrect reading:

- ▶ misinterpretation
- ▶ predisposition
- ▶ unsound reasoning
- ▶ casual reading

Go back and look at the multiple-choice questions. Can you recognize the choice that is a misinterpretation? A predisposition? An unsound reasoning? A too casual reading?

Before we look at the open-ended questions it is important to understand just what the criteria are that will measure the responses. Unlike multiple-choice answers, open-ended questions can have a variety of answer possibilities.

Generally, the guidelines for scoring are very generalized and students can earn 1 to 4 points for a response. Look at the following guidelines for scoring:

**0 points** = short, vague, undeveloped response

**1 point** = does not fully answer the question; makes vague or incorrect, or no reference to the story. The student clearly did not understand the question or the reading.

**2 points** = answers the question but uses confused details from the story; is partially correct but doesn't provide a complete response. The student understood the story and has details from the story to use but has a hard time connecting details to the question being asked.

**3 points** = answers the question and uses details accurately. The student clearly understands the story and the question and can put the two together.

**4 points** = answers the question and uses details accurately; demonstrates insight and understanding. The student not only understands the story and can answer the question with details but also demonstrates insight and the ability to provide a creative answer.

What do open-ended questions and possible high school responses look like? Look at the following questions and the answer/explanations that follow.

### OPEN-ENDED QUESTIONS

1. The story reveals that Miss Brill goes to the park regularly—she goes at the same time every Sunday, sits in the same "special" seat, and gets the same treat each time on her way home. But this time, she does not get a slice of honey cake. Something has changed. What happens to Miss Brill in this story to make her disrupt her routine? What has she learned about herself from this experience? Use details from the story to support your response.

2. The story begins with Miss Brill taking the fur out of its box and ends with her putting the fur back into the box. Early in the story, she imagines the fur asking, "What has been happening to me?" At the end of the story, she imagines that the fur is crying. Why is the fur so important to Miss Brill? What might the fur symbolize?

### OPEN-ENDED QUESTION SAMPLE RESPONSES

**Question 1—Score 0 Response:** *Routines are very important in our lives, especially in the lives of young children. They help us feel safe and secure, and Ms. Brill knows this.*

**Evaluation:** Though this response mentions both routines and Miss Brill, the response is extremely general and underdeveloped. It does not fulfill the assignment or discuss the text.

**Question 1—Score 1 Response:** *Miss Brill has learned from this experience that she should not listen in on other people's conversations. Doing so will only get your feelings hurt. She wouldn't have ruined her lovely day if she hadn't listened to the young couple.*

**Evaluation:** This response merits a slightly higher score because it does fulfill at least part of the assignment—it addresses the question of what Miss Brill has learned. However, this response is also very underdeveloped, and it does not address the other aspects of the assignment. It also offers only a general reference to the text.

**Question 1—Score 2 Response:** *The young couple has made Miss Brill feel like she needs a change of pace. She does the same old thing all the time and she's no longer in fashion. She figures she can start breaking her old routine by first not eating cake like usual, and when she goes home she puts away the fur. Like she's saying goodbye to that "old" Ms. Brill. Now she can start new.*

**Evaluation:** This answer addresses both questions in the assignment, so it is a more satisfactory answer. However, again, the response lacks development. There are good ideas here, but they need more discussion and specific references to the text. Further, there's evidence of some misunderstanding of the story, since Miss Brill most likely did not bypass the bakery simply to break her old routine.

**Question 1—Score 3 Response:** *I think Miss Brill learns that she lives in her own world. She has no real friends, no one to talk to, nothing to do. So she goes to the park by herself to sit silently and listen (though she pretends not to) to what's happening in other people's lives.*

*Miss Brill used to treat herself each week and if she got an almond in her cake, it was like "a tiny present" that really made her day. That treat and watching people in the park seem like the only exciting things she has in her life.*

*I think Miss Brill realizes that though her life is full of people who she watches all day long, her life is actually very empty. She watches all those people, but she doesn't have any connection to them. It's not even that they go in and out of her life; they move around her like she's not there. She's just like one of those silent, staring old people she sees each week who she thinks are so funny. When the boy and girl make fun of her she realizes that she's old and funny, too. And alone.*

*The only "person" Miss Brill actually talks to in the story is her fur. I think she's realized that she needs to have a real person in her life.*

**Evaluation:** This response fulfills all aspects of the assignment correctly and develops each idea. It also refers to specific details in the text, though it does not support all of its assertions with textual evidence.

**Question 1—Score 4 Response:** *Miss Brill is a regular in the park. She left home "at just the same time each week—so as not to be late for the performance." She loves watching the people, taking in all of the action, and even judging the characters in the "play." Before* *the event that changes her, she calls the other regulars "odd" and "silent" and says "there was something funny about nearly all of them." She even says, "from the way they stared they looked as though they'd just come from dark little rooms or even—even cupboards!"*

*Miss Brill spends a lot of time noticing what the other people in the park wear, too—she even notices that the conductor has a new jacket. So when the young couple calls her old and funny and laugh at her fur—which she is so fond of and which she felt so good about wearing—something important happens to Miss Brill. She realizes that she is just like the other regulars who are not part of the action but part of the scenery. Like her, they sit and look and listen, but they don't talk to anyone and don't take part in the play.*

*Miss Brill says that she's "really quite expert" at "listening as though she didn't listen," at "sitting in on other people's lives just for a minute while they talked round her." But she realizes that just listening isn't enough. Just watching and listening has made her a lonely, sad old woman.*

*I think Miss Brill realizes that her routine keeps her shut up in a "dark little room" even when she's outside in the music and light.*

**Evaluation:** This response completely fulfills the assignment and demonstrates a sophisticated and insightful understanding of the text. It is well developed and uses quotes from the text throughout to support its ideas.

**Question 2—Score 0 Response:** *Furs used to be worn a lot more than they are today, because of animal rights groups protesting furs. Ms Brill loved her fur.*

**Evaluation:** This response discusses furs, but not in the context of the story or in the manner requested by the assignment. The student states that Miss Brill loved her fur, but she does not discuss *why* Miss Brill loved her fur. Further, how much furs are worn now and in Miss Brill's time and animal rights groups are completely off-topic.

**Question 2—Score 1 Response:** *The fur must have cost her a lot of money and she is very proud of it. It symbolizes money and power that she wishes she had. She's not happy with her life.*

**Evaluation:** This response attempts to answer the question of why the fur was so important to Miss Brill and what the fur might symbolize, but it is extremely underdeveloped and the ideas are not supported by evidence from the text. The assertions the writer makes, moreover, demonstrate a poor understanding of the story.

**Question 2—Score 2 Response:** *Miss Brill imagines that her fur is alive so that she can feel a little less lonely. She lives alone and the fur gives her someone to talk to. She probably talks to the fur all the time. Maybe it is a symbol of the true love she never had in her life.*

*Miss Brill is sad at the end of the story because the boy and girl made fun of her "friend." The fur cries at the end because its feelings have been hurt, and Miss Brill feels bad about putting it away again. But she's embarrassed, and she will probably never wear the fur again. She's very upset by the kid's criticism.*

**Evaluation:** This response addresses all of the requirements of the assignment and demonstrates a better understanding of the story. However, the response is still underdeveloped and it does not use the text to support its assertions. It also is slightly flawed in its explanations.

**Question 2—Score 3 Response:** *The story "Miss Brill" revolves around the fur. It begins with Miss Brill taking it out of the box and ends with her putting it back in the box. In between, a very important event occurs. A young couple makes fun of Miss Brill and her fur.*

*Because the fur is so important to Miss Brill, this event really shatters her. The fur seems to help her feel good about herself. She says, "it was nice to feel it again" and it gave her a "tingling" feeling to wear it. It makes her feel good to make the fur look good again.*

*I think the fur symbolizes Miss Brill. It's old and a little lifeless. It lives in a box like Miss Brill lives in her little room. It also looks funny to others, like the other regulars in the park look funny to her.*

*Miss Brill thinks the fur is crying in the end but of course it's really Miss Brill who's crying. She realizes that she's not really accepted. Certainly she's no longer fashionable—she's out of date, like her fur.*

**Evaluation:** This response fulfills all aspects of the assignment correctly and develops each idea. It also refers to specific details in the text, though it does not support all of its assertions with textual evidence. The second paragraph is the strongest because it uses quotes from the text to support its ideas.

**Question 2—Score 4 Response:** *By the end of the story, it's clear that Miss Brill's fur is a symbol of Miss Brill herself. In the beginning, she takes the fur out of the box and primps it up, just like she primps herself up to come out of her box (her "dark little room"). Like Miss Brill, the fur is old. Though she says it's the fur who wonders "What has been happening to me?" it's Miss Brill who's wondering what's happening to her, how her life got to be this way. Why has she been shut up in a box for so long? This "box" is Miss Brill's*

*closed-up, lonely world, where she only listens but doesn't talk with others. She may "act,"
but she doesn't interact.*

*Miss Brill's eyes, like the fur's, are sad. She's glad to put the fur on and thinks it will
keep her safe from the "faint chill" in the air, but the fur is dead, like Miss Brill's past,
from where the fur came. It can't protect her.*

*The fur also represents Miss Brill's youth. She is critical of the "ermine toque" who
bought her hat "when her hair was yellow." The condition of Miss Brill's fur tells us that
she bought it (or was given it) a long time ago, too, before her hair was gray. Maybe in
those days she was a "little rogue" herself. But those days are gone. That's the kind of sadness Miss Brill feels—nostalgia. She wants to return to the past. But she can't, and that's
why the fur brings her more sadness.*

*At the end of the story, Miss Brill returns to her "box" and puts the fur back into its
box, too. But this may be a good sign. Maybe Miss Brill has realized that the past is the
past and that she cannot be what she used to be.*

*I think that what Miss Brill needs to do is realize that she doesn't have to grow old
alone. There are plenty of old "furs" out there, sitting alone in their rooms "like cupboards," waiting for someone to come into their lives.*

**Evaluation:** This response completely fulfills the assignment and demonstrates a
sophisticated and insightful understanding of the text. It is well developed and uses
quotes from the text throughout to support its ideas. In addition, it concludes with
a thoughtful judgment of the character that connects the story to our real lives.

### READING CONSUMER DOCUMENTS AND NONFICTION

Are you getting a better idea of just what the new, higher standards are? Well, you've
just looked at a sample of a reading comprehension question based on narrative text.
That is, the kind of reading that a student might do in English class. But today's reading comprehension goes way beyond just reading literature. Remember we mentioned
earlier "consumer" documents and nonfiction? Let's take a look at what reading consumer information, or general nonfiction, might look like.

On a recent New York State Comprehensive English Regents Examination, students
were given the following "situation" to respond to:

The planning team in your school is interested in developing a school-to-
work program in connection with businesses in your community. As a member of the career guidance class, you have been asked to write a letter to the

school planning team in which you describe the benefits of school-to-work programs and the conditions needed to make such programs successful.

They were then asked to examine two documents related to the question. The first was a graph from the National Employer Survey, administered by the U.S. Bureau of the Census, in 1994. The second was an essay on school-to-work programs. There were then 10 multiple-choice questions specific to the graph and the text that helped students identify key ideas to use when they wrote their letter to the school planning team.

The test's specific directions required students to use relevant information from both documents in their letters and the following guidelines were given:

- ▶ Tell your audience what they need to know about the benefits of school-to-work programs and the conditions needed to make such programs successful.
- ▶ Use specific, accurate, and relevant information from the text and graph to support your discussion.
- ▶ Use a tone and level of language appropriate for a letter to the school planning team.
- ▶ Organize your ideas in a logical and coherent manner.
- ▶ Indicate any words taken directly from the text by using quotation marks or referring to the author.
- ▶ Follow the conventions of standard written English.

This task skillfully combined reading comprehension with a more elaborated writing response. Students had to write a full length essay to demonstrate their ability to read with precision and understanding. They also had to be able to choose and then reformulate selected information to suit a specified rhetorical purpose. Their work was graded (evaluated) against a set of criteria that looked something like the chart on the next page.

The diagram on the next page is called a criteria chart or a rubric, and it spells out the guidelines for scoring a response. This particular rubric runs horizontally and the score of "4" or "A" is described in the boxes at the top. "3" or "B" is represented in the second row. "2" or "C" is represented in the third row. "1" or "D" is represented in the fourth row. "0" or "F" would be a totally illegible or off task paper.

There are certain criteria that are basic to all writing tasks. Listed below are the five most basic criteria:

- ▶ Establish a focus by asserting a main or controlling idea.
- ▶ Develop content using sufficient and appropriate supporting details.

| | FOCUS | CONTENT | ORGANIZATION | STYLE | CONVENTIONS |
|---|---|---|---|---|---|
| 4 | Sharp, distinct, controlling main point made about the topic with evident awareness of task; chooses strong and compelling evidence from both documents to support point of view. | Substantial, specific and/or illustrative content demonstrating development and support of the topic. | Sophisticated arrangement of content into clearly developed paragraphs with appropriate transitions. | Careful choice of words and sentence structure to support and highlight purpose and tone. | None or only one or two errors in grammar, spelling, or sentence usage. |
| 3 | Apparent main point made about the topic with sufficient awareness of task; adequate choice of supporting details from the two documents. | Sufficiently developed content with adequate use of details related to the main idea. | Adequate arrangement of content into paragraphs which follow the main idea; some transitions. | Adequate choice of words; basic but repeated sentence structure. | Errors in grammar, spelling, usage that do not interfere with communication of ideas. |
| 2 | The topic is identified but no main point is established and only one document is referred to; weak choice of supporting information or supporting information does not apply to point made. | Limited content; details not all related to main idea. | Confused arrangement of content; paragraphs do not establish a logical pattern of organization; no transitions. | Poor choice of vocabulary; weak but grade appropriate sentence structure. | Errors in grammar, spelling, usage somewhat interfere with communication. |
| 1 | Minimal evidence of topic; no main idea; no use of supporting evidence from documents. | No details specific to a main idea; no explanation of details as they relate to topic. | No control of paragraphs; no transitions. | Poor choice of vocabulary; weak and grade inappropriate sentence structure. | Errors in grammar, spelling, usage interfere with communication. |

- ▶ Provide a logical pattern of organization with appropriate transitions and well-developed paragraphs.
- ▶ Convey a sense of style with the use of varied and effective sentences, with the tone appropriate to the task and audience, and with effective diction.
- ▶ Control the conventions of standard written English including usage, mechanics, and sentence sense.

These criteria are then defined according to a specific task. For example, in the chart you just read, using information from the two documents was a critical requirement so it appears as criteria for grading.

The previous task required students to use two pieces of information on which to base a full-length essay response. Many states use only one persuasive or expository piece for students. Consider the following persuasive essay about the rights of student athletes. Students will be asked to read the essay and then, just like the narrative piece above, they will answer 10 multiple-choice questions and write two open-ended responses. The major difference is the nature of the reading assignment. It is a persuasive, nonfiction piece, not a piece of literature.

## *The Rights of Child Athletes*
### *by Dr. Denise Wood*

The number of children who are participating in organized youth sports is increasing. Children from five to sixteen years old are participating in sports sponsored by schools, communities, and clubs. Sports participation offers many benefits for children physically, mentally, and emotionally. The well-being of children should be the main objective of their participation in sports. As athletes, children have rights that must be respected and protected by the adults who structure the sport environment.

First, children have the right to participate in organized sports to have fun. Sports and games are exciting and challenging. Children enjoy building friendships by cooperating with teammates as well as by competing against opponents. They like to express themselves through activities. Sports participation should be a rewarding experience for children. Sports should not be a source of negative experiences for them. The most important reason why children participate in organized youth sports is to have fun.

Second, children have the right to play a role in making decisions with their parents concerning how early in life they should participate in sports. Sometimes children pressure their parents to let them participate in sports because their friends or older siblings are involved in organized sports. While young children may think they will have fun, they may not be ready for organized competition.

Also, parents may pressure children into participating in sports at a very young age because parents want their children to get a head start in sports. Parents want to encourage their children to learn skills as early as possible. Parents occasionally want their children to engage in a particular sport so that they can live out their own dreams through their children. Children should not be pressured into competition prematurely. However, children have the right to participate in decision making about their own sports participation. Together, children, parents, coaches, and other qualified adults should decide whether or not children are ready to compete in organized youth sports.

Third, children have the right to be safe and protected from injury in organized sports participation. According to the U.S. Consumer Product Safety Commission, over one million children age 14 and under are treated for sports-related injuries in hospital emergency rooms each year. Many of these injuries could be prevented or minimized through proper training and equipment.

Overuse injuries are becoming much more common than in the past. Injuries such as little league elbow, swimmer's shoulder, and gymnast's back were seldom heard of prior to the rise of organized youth sports. Experts believe that the increase in the incidence of overuse injuries among children is due to: (a) the growth of organized youth sports and the number of children who are participating, (b) countless hours of training and competition at an early age, and (c) year round participation in sports. Children are more vulnerable to overuse injuries than adults because their bones are in the growth process.

Sports will never be injury free, but there are many precautions that can be taken to limit the number and severity of injuries. Protective eyewear, facemasks, mouth guards, shin guards, and other types of safety gear and support devices greatly reduce the likelihood and severity of injuries. Facilities should be free from obstacles and other hazards that could cause injuries. Adults should be sensitive to early symptoms of overuse injuries and get medical attention for children as early as possible. Some experts recommend that children not participate in any sport more than five days per week and avoid year round sports participation. Children trust that parents, coaches, administrators, and officials will protect them from injuries. Adults should respect the right of children to be safe and take steps to help them avoid injuries due to sports competition.

Fourth, children have the right to have qualified adult leadership when they participate in organized sports. Coaches of organized youth sport teams should take responsibility to not only be knowledgeable about the skills and strategies of a sport, but to also know principles of training and conditioning for the sport. They should be aware of the social and psychological impact of competition on children. Coaches should provide strong leadership and be positive role models. Children learn more from coaches by the example that coaches set than by what coaches say. Good sportsmanship, fair play, and cooperation are only a few qualities that children can develop through sports by observing the desirable attitudes and behaviors of their coaches.

Children rely on their parents to provide guidance and support whether they win or lose. Parents can place a great deal of stress on children to succeed. Children are concerned that their parents will not love them if they disappoint their parents by losing. Parents must let their children know that they love them and are proud of them regardless of their performance. Children learn spectator behavior from their parents. It is critical that parents also stand as positive role models for their children if children are to reap the benefits of participation.

Fifth, children have a right to participate with other athletes of similar capabilities. Coaches should strive to match athletes according to their skill and experience, as well as their height, weight, age, and level of maturity. Mismatching child athletes has many undesirable effects. Smaller athletes are more vulnerable to injury if overpowered by larger athletes. Older children are likely to have the advantage of experience as well as size over younger athletes. Greater skill levels, more knowledge and use of strategies, and readiness to learn are benefits for older, more mature athletes. Children have the right to participate in sports with other children who provide fair and equal competition.

Adults should respect the rights of children when they participate as athletes in organized youth sports. In addition to the five rights that have already been noted, children should be provided equal opportunities to strive for success and they should be treated with dignity. Most importantly, children have the right to have fun!

**MULTIPLE-CHOICE QUESTIONS**

1.  Which of the following BEST describes the central idea of this article?
    a.  Coaches are not qualified to protect child athletes from injuries.
    b.  Children who participate in organized youth sports have rights.
    c.  Parents should encourage their children to participate in sports.
    d.  Organized youth sports can be dangerous.

2.  Which of the following best describes the author's attitude toward children's participation in organized youth sports?
    a.  antagonistic and angry
    b.  indifferent and nonchalant
    c.  suspicious and apprehensive
    d.  protective and concerned

3.  "Overuse injuries" are those injuries that occur because
    a.  the same motion executed repeatedly over time causes damage.
    b.  children do not warm up properly.
    c.  children do not wear the proper protective equipment.
    d.  sports are too violent for children.

4.  In order to be persuasive, the author uses all of the following EXCEPT
    a.  statistics.
    b.  emotion.
    c.  reason.
    d.  examples.

5.  By behaving as good role models, coaches can teach children
    a.  to improve sport skills.
    b.  to avoid injuries.
    c.  proper training techniques.
    d.  good sportsmanship.

6.  Who would most likely use this article to support their position?
    a.  school superintendents
    b.  children's rights advocates
    c.  sports equipment salespeople
    d.  recreation center directors

7. Which of the following BEST describes the organization of the text?
   a. chronological order
   b. order of importance
   c. pro and con order
   d. easy to difficult order

8. All of the following are reasons why children should not be mismatched when participating in organized youth sports EXCEPT
   a. coaches are legally liable for injuries.
   b. smaller children could get hurt.
   c. the self-worth of older children is boosted.
   d. children should be given equal competition.

9. Who would the author most want to read this article?
   a. sports equipment manufacturers
   b. facilities maintenance crews
   c. older brothers and sisters
   d. parents and coaches

10. A concern that children have if they do not win is that
   a. they will think that their parents will not love them.
   b. they will lose their friends.
   c. their coaches will hit them.
   d. they will not be able to compete when they get older.

### ANSWERS AND EXPLANATIONS—MULTIPLE-CHOICE QUESTIONS

1. **b.** The central idea of this article is that children have rights when they participate in organized youth sports. The idea was originally introduced in the first paragraph, expanded upon and supported throughout the body, and reinforced in the closing.

2. **d.** The article concerns the rights of children and indicates that adults are responsible for respecting the rights of children and protecting them. The author repeatedly refers to behaviors that adults should display that advocate protection and concern.

3. **a.** The term "overuse injuries" is never defined. It must be understood through context. In addition to the meaning that the term implies, paragraph six, "count-

less hours of training and competition" and "year round participation in sports," provides clues as to the meaning.

4. **d.** A statistic (**a**) is cited (over one million children age 14 and under per year visiting emergency rooms) in paragraph five. Emotions (**b**) are appealed to through use of terms such as "rights," "responsibilities," and "must be protected" in each paragraph. Reason (**c**) is repeatedly used to support each right of children. No examples are ever used to reveal a specific incident where a child's rights were violated.

5. **d.** The use of the term "behaving" in the stem, as well as the use of "role model" in paragraph eight concerning coaches, indicate that **d** is the correct answer. In paragraph eight, the social and psychological impacts of sports are mentioned. Therefore, one example of positive role modeling that coaches can provide is good sportsmanship.

6. **b.** The title of the article, as well as the repeated references to the rights of children in each paragraph, indicates that **b** is the correct answer. As responsible adults, school superintendents, sports equipment salespeople, and recreation center directors should be concerned about the rights of children. However, the best answer is **b,** children's rights advocates, because the article is specifically directed toward children's rights as they relate to sports.

7. **b.** There are no dates listed in the passage, so **a** is eliminated. There is little presentation of cons in this persuasive passage, so **c** is eliminated. There are no levels of difficulty, so **d** is eliminated. Therefore, **b,** order of importance, is correct because "fun" was indicated as the first and primary reason for children to participate and should be protected. The passage reveals other rights in some detail, and then additional rights of less importance. The primary right, to have fun, was noted again in the last sentence.

8. **c.** Paragraph ten clearly indicates that the other options do apply as reasons why children should be equally matched. There is no reference to the self worth of older children being boosted as a reason to match children of equal characteristics. On the contrary, this might be a result of mismatching. The stem says EXCEPT, so **c** is the correct answer.

9. **d.** The entire article appeals to parents and coaches, who are the primary responsible adults who structure the sport environment. They are held accountable for protecting the rights of children throughout the article.

10. **a.** Paragraph nine contains this sentence: "Children are concerned that their parents will not love them if they disappoint their parents by losing." There is no mention of losing friends, coaches hitting them, or not being able to compete

when they get older as a consequence of their performance. Therefore, **a** is the correct answer.



1.  The author writes, "Sports participation offers many benefits for children physically, mentally, and emotionally."
    - Participation in sports has some obvious benefits for children physically. How can sports participation benefit children mentally and emotionally? Please explain.
    - Give an example from your own experience or observation to support your explanation.

    Use information from the passage to support your response.

2.  The author of this passage expresses concern for the right of children to be protected from physical injuries that can occur from sports participation. Yet, over one million children per year are treated in emergency rooms for injuries that they receive in sports.
    - If so many children are treated for injuries each year, are parents failing to protect children's right to be safe? Please explain your answer.
    - Give examples of how parents can help prevent or minimize physical injuries for their children who participate in organized youth sports.

    Use information from the passage to support your response.

## OPEN-ENDED SAMPLE RESPONSES

**Question 1—Score 0 Response:** *Sports are fun to play. Kids can get out and run around. I can run much faster now than I could before I played basketball. Basketball is a great sport. I'm glad I went out for it.*

**Evaluation:** This response is irrelevant and off-topic. It is not focused on the task. There is no reference to the mental and emotional benefits of sports other than sports being fun to play.

**Question 1—Score 1 Response:** *Being in a sport helps children learn how to get along with others. They have to play like a team. They cannot win if they do not work well together. They have to cooperate with each other by giving up the ball and not hogging it. If they hog the ball, the team could lose.*

**Evaluation:** There is minimal understanding of this task. There is mention of getting along with others and of teamwork. There is a vague reference to the text concerning cooperation. The requirements of the task are not completed because there is little explanation and no specific example.

**Question 1—Score 2 Response:** *Sport participation can benefit children mentally and emotionally because they have to learn how to play without getting mad. They have to learn how to be good sports if they lose. They have to practice more and do better the next time. My brother now takes more vitamins so he can get stronger because he does not want to lose. His team has not done very well this year. If he takes vitamins, he may not lose as much and then he will not be mad as much.*

**Evaluation:** The requirements of the task have been addressed in that the response includes an explanation of how sports can benefit children mentally and emotionally. The response uses "without getting mad" as a way that children can benefit from sports other than physically. There is an explanation and an example using a brother and his actions. The explanation is flawed and inconsistent because taking vitamins and getting stronger do not relate to the brother's benefiting from sports participation emotionally or mentally.

**Question 1—Score 3 Response:** *Sports can help children grow emotionally and mentally because they have to learn to play fairly, get along with other children, and show good sportsmanship. Every player on a team must work together with their teammates if the team is going to win. If a call goes against them, they have to accept it without arguing. If they lose, they have to congratulate the opposing team and show good sportsmanship.*

*When I played softball when I was 12, I learned that I had to cooperate with other girls on my team whether I liked them or not. We had a good team because we learned to play well with each other and put other personal issues aside. We always had to play by the rules so that if we won, we knew that we won fairly. If we lost a game, the coach always made us shake hands with the other team and show respect to them because they won fairly.*

**Evaluation:** The response demonstrates that the student understands the task. All of the requirements are met. The student addresses fair play, cooperation, and good sportsmanship as ways that children can benefit from sports emotionally and mentally. She expands on each of them generally by giving examples. Finally, she gives specific examples of how she and her teammates benefited emotionally and mentally. She uses examples from the text from paragraph eight.

**Question 1—Score 4 Response:** *Sports can be beneficial to children in many ways, including mentally and emotionally. Paragraph eight says, "Good sportsmanship, fair play, and* *cooperation are only a few qualities that children can develop through sport by observing the desirable attitudes and behaviors of their coaches." Children can learn from their experiences in sports that can help them in other areas of their lives outside of sports. For example, when children learn how to play fairly by the rules of the game, they learn how to follow rules when they are in class or out in public. They learn in sports that cooperating with the coach and with teammates for the good of the team is what will help them win. If they can cooperate with teammates in sports to win games, they can successfully complete group projects in school or community projects. If they can graciously accept losing as well as winning in their sport, they can learn to be good sports if they win or lose a spelling bee.*

*I did not participate in sports as a child, but I noticed that my friends who played sports seemed to learn how to work well with me and other children on projects. For example, when we worked together on a school play one of my friends, Joey, who played soccer, told everyone how important they were no matter what their role was. He said we would make the play a success if everyone did their part well and if anyone had trouble he said that we would all pitch in to help. He said that if we listened to the director and encouraged each other to do our best, that we would have an outstanding production, and we did. I think it was because Joey played soccer for a long time that he knew that if we all cooperated and supported each other, that we would succeed. This is an example of how children can benefit mentally and emotionally from their participation in sports.*

**Evaluation:** This student clearly demonstrates understanding of the task. All of the requirements are completed. A clear explanation of how children can benefit mentally and emotionally is provided. Examples of how children can apply sports experiences beyond the sport extends aspects of the text in paragraph eight. The example of how Joey used his experience in sports to support other children and to cooperate with each other to make a school play successful provides an insightful example from personal observation.

**Question 2—Score 0 Response:** *Children can get hurt in sports if they are not careful. Parents have to take them to the hospital when they get hurt. Lots of kids I know have had to go to the doctor. They end up with scars and sometimes they are proud of their scars.*

**Evaluation:** The response is irrelevant and does not address the task requirement. There is no mention of parents failing to protect their children's right to be safe and there are no examples of how injuries can be prevented or minimized.

**Question 2—Score 1 Response:** *Millions of children get injured each year by playing sports. Their parents have not protected them. They did not get them the proper equip-*

*ment and they got injured. Parents could have gotten them shin guards or other equipment, but they did not. This is how so many children get injured each year.*

**Evaluation:** The response demonstrates that the student has some understanding of the task, but does not complete the requirements. It does not explain whether or not parents and coaches are protecting children's right to be safe. There is one reference to the text (use of shin guards) concerning how injuries can be prevented.

**Question 2—Score 2 Response:** *Children's rights are not being protected. Parents are not protecting their children very well if over one million of them per year end up in emergency rooms. Parents must not be getting them the right equipment. Children may be playing on teams where coaches are keeping kids in games when they are beginning to get an injury and playing hard makes it so bad that they have to go to the hospital.*

*My cousin said that his shoulder hurt him quite a bit and his parents made him play anyway. He really never liked playing even before he hurt his shoulder. He finally quit playing last year.*

**Evaluation:** All of the requirements of the task are met, but understanding of the task is partial. The student offers an answer to the question concerning whether or not parents are not protecting children. There is a brief explanation that refers to the text (the right equipment, responsible coaches). The statistic from the text is cited, but the logic is flawed in that the student does not consider other explanations and concludes that parents are not protecting children. An example of the student's cousin and his injury is mentioned. However, the example does not relate back to the issue of parents protecting children.

**Question 2—Score 3 Response:** *Parents are probably not protecting their children's right to be safe to the extent that they could be. Many parents do not spend time with their children at practices or at games. Some do not look into what the best equipment to protect them would be. They sometimes leave that up to the coaches, assuming that the coaches are qualified and knowledgeable about equipment. They also trust that coaches know everything that they should about conditioning and training children properly. Some coaches of organized youth sports have no formal training to coach children. They rely on their own previous experience as athletes. Parents may not question coaches about many of the safety precautions that should be taken so that their children do not get injured.*

*Parents can help to prevent or minimize injuries by finding out what equipment is going to protect their children the best in any given sport. They should be sure that their children have all of the protective equipment that they need to be as safe as possible. They should be sure that there are enough qualified coaches. Parents can check on the coaches' credentials to be sure that the coaches are capable of coaching young children correctly. Par-*

*ents should make sure that their children are not playing in more than two sports and not participating more than five times per week.*

**Evaluation:** This response demonstrates completion of all task requirements and provides original ideas and ideas from the text to support points. The student refers to the need for safety equipment and qualified coaches who can provide proper training (paragraph eight). The student gives examples of why some coaches may not be qualified and what parents can do to help ensure that coaches have the proper qualifications, which can limit the number of injuries. Recommendations are drawn from paragraph seven concerning how often and during how much of the year children should participate.

**Question 2—Score 4 Response:** *As indicated in paragraph five, "over one million children age 14 and under are treated for sports-related injuries in hospital emergency rooms each year. Many of these injuries could be prevented or minimized through proper training and equipment."*

*This figure seems quite high; however, it does not indicate the total of how many children across the country are competing in organized youth sports, including the number who do visit emergency rooms. It also does not indicate whether or not the same children are seen repeatedly or in which sports they participate. It may be that some children who sustain injuries are from lower income families or communities. They may not be able to afford to buy the best equipment and less expensive equipment may not serve to protect children from injuries to a great extent. It may be that only certain sports are known to produce more injuries. It may also be that coaches are not qualified. They may not be knowledgeable about proper training and conditioning, which will help to prevent injuries among children who participate in sports.*

*The article does not provide sufficient information or evidence to come to any conclusions to the question. Therefore, my answer to the question, "If so many children are treated for injuries each year, are parents failing to protect their children's right to be safe" is that it is my opinion that adults are making efforts to protect the rights of children to be safe. I believe that steps have been taken in many sports that require the use of equipment with specific safety standards. More and more coaches are being certified in their respective sports. Parents, overall, are concerned about the welfare of their children. As indicated in paragraph 7, sports will never be injury free. There is always a risk of injury even when every effort has been made to keep children safe. I believe that overall parents and coaches are successful in protecting children's right to be safe.*

*There are many ways that injuries due to participation in organized youth sports can be prevented or minimized. Paragraph six indicates that, "Protective eye wear, face masks, mouth guards, shin guards, and other types of safety gear and support devices greatly reduce the likelihood and severity of injuries. Facilities should be free from obstacles and other hazards which could cause injuries." Other examples of protective devices include the use of mats and padding for gymnastics, helmets for baseball and football, knee and ankle wraps for weightlifting, and arch supports in shoes that are used in a variety of sports.*

*Other ways to prevent or minimize injuries include engaging in adequate warm up exercises to prepare for more strenuous sport activity. These exercises involve aerobic activities as well as flexibility exercises to prevent muscle strains and related injuries. Sport training should include conditioning exercises to strengthen muscles so joints are more stable and less likely to be affected by forceful impacts.*

**Evaluation:** This response clearly completes the requirements of the tasks. Specific parts of the task are repeated and sections of the text are quoted or paraphrased. Insightful explanations are provided from the student's own knowledge and experience. The question of whether or not parents are protecting the right of children to be safe is answered clearly. The statistic that over one million children per year visit emergency rooms is questioned and alternative explanations are provided as to why this statistic seems so high.

### STAND-ALONE WRITING

The previous examples of reading and writing are called *text-based* questions. That is, they rely on students to read and base their answers on what they have read. But there is another type of writing question that requires students to write without the benefit of text to support them. This kind of writing is called *stand-alone* and it means exactly what it says. The writing stands apart from text and requires the student to rely on his or her personal experience or ideas about a given topic. It also requires that a student be able to read the question, outline notes, formulate an organized response, and prepare a finished, complete, and almost error free piece of writing in a timed setting. A student must have had many such experiences in the classroom and at home to be able to accomplish this successfully.

There are two main types of stand-alone writing: narrative and persuasive.

Let's take the following example of a persuasive writing task which might be found on any state's high school exit exam.

Across the country, more and more public schools are requiring students to comply with dress codes. Those who support dress codes say that there are fewer problems in their schools. Those who are against dress codes say that it takes away from their individuality.

Should schools require students to conform to a prescribed dress code? Write a letter to the superintendent of your school district to convince him or her why there should/should not be a dress code for students in your school. Support your argument with at least 3 good reasons for your position.

The stand-alone prompt is considered a full-length essay and is generally scored on a 1–6 scale. The writing counts for more than the open-ended response because the essay is longer and is expected to be a fully developed piece of writing that demonstrates that the writer is aware of introductions and conclusions, organization patterns such as cause/effect, order of importance, comparison/contrast, logical organization, paragraphing, and transitions. The writer is expected to demonstrate a sense of audience and purpose through word choice and tone. In other words, the full-length essay is expected to be a carefully constructed piece of some length.

Let's examine some responses to the dress code task.

## Inadequate Command—1 Point:

*Dear Mr. Jonsen,*
*I like my own clothes. No body can say how i look. Some like to dress diffrent from me, some guys do how they want and i do how i want. Can't all ware the same thing.*

**Evaluation:** This response demonstrates an inadequate command and would receive a grade of 1. The content and organization of this response show no definite opening or closing that address the task of writing a letter to convince the superintendent of the author's position on dress codes. The response is very brief and unfocused. The author has not provided three reasons to support his or her argument. It does not appear that the author has planned his or her response very well. There are numerous errors in usage, including slang. Except for the first sentence, the other sentences are incomplete or incorrect and contain several errors in sentence structure. Mechanical errors include punctuation, spelling, and capitalization.

## Limited Command—2 Points:

*Dear Mr. Smith:*
*A dress code is no good. One reasin is, I got to have clothes that are me. Not nobody else. Every-body has do they own thing. Also, wrong colors make trouble but it is really you. Same clothes make you look all a like not different. No body should be like every body else. Styles importint. Princpls shoun't make you dress like the other ones.*

**Evaluation:** This response shows limited command of the English language and would receive a grade of 2. The author provides a thesis sentence for the opening and initially focuses on the task by providing reasons for his or her position, but does not complete the task. There is some attempt at organization, but the response lacks detail and is repetitive. There are numerous errors in usage and some sentences are incomplete and use the same brief, repetitive structure. There are errors in spelling and punctuation.


## Partial Command—3 Points:

*Dear Dr. Simpson,*
*Some kids parents don't have enough to by expensive stuff and they don't feel good about it. Having to wear the same cloths would make them not stand out. Then rich kids would not think that they are better than poor ones. An other reason is that you couldn't get beat up by gangs. Gangs have certain colors that you can't wear the wrong color or you could get into trouble with them. If we all have the same colors no one knows who is in a gang. The dress code clothes do not cost so much as designer ones mostly. Some people have to get jobs to just to get in clothes and be accepted. It costs too much to get them. Nobody wants to pay so much just to look good in school. I think we need a dress code in our school.*

**Evaluation:** This response shows partial command of the English language and would receive a grade of 3. The opening statement does not relate to the task. The closing statement is focused on the task most of the time. However, the author shows a lapse in organization by referring back to the first reason after noting a second reason. Some errors exist in usage and there is little variety and some errors in sentence construction. Some errors in spelling and punctuation are evident.


## Adequate Command—4 Points:

*Dear Dr. Wilson,*
*I have heard that our school might have a dress code and we would all have to wear certain kinds of clothes. I like that idea.*

*One reason is that some people think they are better than others because of how they dress. Some kids have designer clothes and think their so good and others don't because they don't like them or can't afford them. Just because they have lots of money doesn't mean their better than anyone else. Some people look down on others because of how they dress and having a dress code might stop them from thinking that their so good.*

*Another reason I think a dress code is good is because it would help everyone feel like they belong. Some people who don't have much money would think they belong as much as those who do.*

*The third reason is that it would stop some students from wearing some types of clothes that do not look so good. Some boys wear pants so lose that it shows too much too low. Some girls wear such short tops and it shows their stomachs. If there was a dress code, they couldn't wear clothes that cause problems.*

**Evaluation:** This response shows adequate command of the English language and would receive a grade of 4. There is a clear opening, but it lacks a strong closing; the essay just ends after the third reason. The author provides three reasons, but confuses connection between the first two. Transitions are evident. The first and third points provide greater elaboration than the second point, indicating uneven development of details. There are a few errors in usage and mechanics, but they do not interfere with the meaning of the essay.


**Strong Command—5 Points:**

*Dear Dr. Kingman,*

*I am writing to you to urge you not to start a dress code in our school. I have very strong feelings on the issue and I hope you will listen to them.*

*The first reason that we should not have a dress code is because it detracts from each student's individuality. Clothes provide a way for us to express ourselves. What we wear tells others how we see ourselves, as well as how we want to be seen. A dress code would mean that we not be able to attract friends who think and dress like we do.*

*The second reason that we should not have a dress code is that we want to be treated like adults. Teachers do not have a dress code so we should not have one either. We are always told to grow up and act like adults. Now we may all have to dress the way the school decides that we should, as if we are small children.*

*The final reason, and the most important, why we should not have a dress code is because it takes away our personal freedom. A dress code would take away our own right to decide what we can wear on our own bodies. This is a free country and we have the freedom to choose the clothes that we want to.*

*I hope that you agree with my position. Please persuade the school board to vote "no" on the dress code.*

*Sincerely yours,*
*Michelle Jenkins*

**Evaluation:** This response demonstrates strong command of the English language and would receive a grade of 5. There is a clear opening and closing. The author provides three reasons for her position on dress codes and she provides supporting evidence for her position, but not at great length. She uses separate paragraphs to identify the reasons for her position. Her response contains a single focus and has sense of unity and coherence. There is also a logical progression of ideas. There are very few errors in sentence construction and mechanics, none of which interfere with the meaning.

## Superior Command—6 Points:

*Dear Dr. Jones,*

*It is my understanding that the Evansville Board of Education is considering implementing a dress code by which students at Evansville High School must comply. I would like to take this opportunity to voice strong support for a dress code for the three major reasons which I will describe in this letter.*

*First, a dress code at Evansville High School would require all students to wear clothing and accessories that are considered to be appropriate standards of attire by the Board of Education. Such standards would allow all students to feel that they are treated equally and not discriminated against by other students based on the clothes that they wear. Students from lower socioeconomic classes cannot afford to dress in designer clothing, while students from higher socioeconomic classes can. The difference in students' ability to afford more expensive designer clothing promotes a distinction between the classes and cause students in lower socioeconomic classes to feel inferior and socially unacceptable. Thus, a dress code would disallow discrimination based on family income.*

*Second, compliance to a dress code would promote a theme of professionalism in our school. Currently, many students wear clothing that is totally unacceptable in an educational institution. If you and the school board wish to instill standards which are acceptable in our professional careers, then we should become accustomed to those standards of our professional lives during high school. The attire that is worn by some of our students would never be tolerated in the workplace. Compliance with a dress code would ensure that our students understand the expectations of dress in their future professions. Therefore, a dress code would contribute to the professional preparation of students at Evansville High School.*

*Third, a dress code would eliminate the potential incidents of violence concerning gang-related activities in our schools and communities. Members of gangs wear specific colors which allow them to be associated with their own gangs. If a student inadvertently wears clothing in the color they prefer, but that color happens to be one adopted by a gang, the student could be attacked when walking outside in the community or even at school. We are all aware of the increase of violence in schools and many of us are afraid to attend school for fear of being attacked or even losing our lives. If you were to require a dress code, students would feel safer and the likelihood of being attacked by gang members would be virtually eliminated.*

*I have cited the main reasons for the implementation of a dress code at Evansville High School. Avoiding discrimination based on socioeconomic class, promoting professional preparation, and taking important steps to ensure the safety of our students are all excellent reasons to implement a dress code. I strongly encourage you and the Evansville School Board to take the responsibility with which you have been charged. Please ensure that a dress code is implemented in our school before the next school year begins.*

*Thank you for your consideration and cooperation concerning this very important issue.*

*Sincerely,*

*Judy Bonds*

**Evaluation:** This response shows a superior command of the English language and would receive a grade of 6. The author provides a clear opening and closing. She gives three reasons for her position on the issue (each in its own paragraph, clearly identified) and provides supporting evidence of her position. Her positions are well developed and transitions are evident throughout the response. The response displays a single, distinct focus, is unified and coherent, and ideas are presented in a logical progression. She summarizes her main points in a paragraph prior to the closing and continues to focus on her position. Sentence construction, usage, and mechanics are virtually flawless.

## KINDS OF WRITING

In addition to persuasive writing, there are two other kinds of writing used on state exams to measure a student's ability to use language effectively. They are narrative and expository writing. Briefly described:

- ▶ Narrative writing asks students to tell a story or recount an event from their personal experiences. They are expected to develop a plot, characters, and a setting. Narrative prompts ask students to *tell* or *relate* and to provide *details*.
- ▶ Expository writing asks students to describe ideas, explain problems, and analyze solutions. Students are asked to *explain* or *describe* and to be *specific*.
- ▶ Persuasive writing asks students to convince readers to agree with their position on a topic. Students are asked to *convince* or *persuade* and be specific in developing an *argument*.

Most high school exit exams use persuasive writing as the basis of the full-length essay. Narrative writing is used on the elementary tests, expository writing is used on the middle school. But that does not mean that any one of these three types of writing cannot or will not be used on an exit exam. Please refer to the narrative and expository examples provided in Chapters 5 and 7 for more specific details about these types of essay.

Where is the literature on these new English/Language Arts assessments? Doesn't English mean literature? After all, that's what kids do in English class. The new ELA assessments are NOT literature based. They are intended to measure a student's ability to read and write effectively for a variety of purposes, and responding to literature is just one of them. Most state ELA assessments deal with literature in the reading comprehension section, when students are asked to read short stories or poems and respond based on the knowledge and experience with literature that they have gained from their English classes. For instance, they are expected to be able to identify literary devices such as metaphors and similes; to recognize point of view; and to determine theme. Rarely will a state ELA exam ask questions specific to a work of literature. Only the end-of-course exams (English) mentioned earlier will rely heavily on literature content.

For example, New York State includes a *Critical Lens* question on its comprehensive exam. This question prompts students to respond to a topic using any two works of literature that they have read. Here's an example:

> Write a critical essay in which you discuss two works of literature you have read from the particular perspective of the statement that is provided for you in the Critical Lens. In your essay, provide a valid interpretation of the statement, agree or disagree with the statements as you have interpreted it, and support your opinion using specific references to appropriate literary elements from the two works. You may use scrap paper to plan your response.

**Critical Lens:**
"All conflict in literature is, in its simplest form, a struggle between good and evil."

Guidelines:
Be sure to

- provide a valid interpretation of the critical lens that clearly establishes the criteria for analysis.
- indicate whether you agree or disagree with the statement as you have interpreted it.
- choose two works you have read that you believe best support your opinion.
- use the criteria suggested by the critical lens to analyze the works you have chosen.

- avoid plot summary. Instead, use specific references to appropriate literary elements (for example: theme, characterization, setting, point of view) to develop your analysis.
- organize your ideas in a unified and coherent manner.
- specify the titles and authors of the literature you choose.
- follow the conventions of standard written English.

This question, though very literature specific, gives students a wide range in selecting works of literature to apply to the question.

There are any number of combinations of question types and rubrics for scoring which vary from state to state. The way to ascertain what your state requires is to visit the website (see Appendix A) and/or ask your child's English teacher or building principal for a copy of a previous exam.

> ☛ **PARENT TIP:** Request that your parents' association sponsor an evening meeting to which you invite a district spokesperson to take you through the actual test(s) that your child must take to get a high school diploma. Arrange a series of meetings by subject area and test so that you can closely examine the questions and exemplar answers. Information is the best guide.

## Accountability

WHILE IT IS very important to hold students to higher and higher levels of performance, make no mistake, your child needs guidance to reach those expectations. State required examinations not only measure students, they also measure schools and teachers.

Your state may have a "Report Card" system for your local school district and its individual schools that shows just how many of the students passed or failed the state tests. Or, you may have to go to a school board meeting and ask for the information. But under the new H.R. 1 legislation, all states must report the following data to the public by the 2002–2003 school year:

- ▶ Student academic achievement on state tests disaggregated by subgroups
- ▶ Comparison of students at basic, proficient, or advanced levels of achievement
- ▶ Graduation rates
- ▶ Number and names of schools designated for improvement
- ▶ Comparison of actual academic achievement levels

▶ Professional qualifications of teachers

▶ Percentage of students not tested

In other words, all school districts must report—to its parents—the results of tests *compared with the results of other schools in the district and even other districts and schools in the state*. This is important information for you to have. If your school or district consistently performs poorly, it may be designated as a school in need of assistance. You may then have other options available to you, such as school choice.

However, the goal of this book is to give you information about the test instruments. Now it's time to look at mathematics for your high school student.

# Looking at High School Exit Exams: Mathematics

**The three** R's: reading, writing, and arithmetic. Long considered the essential skills that drive access to all other areas of learning and communication, reading, writing, and arithmetic are the basics in any state's basic competency program. But just as the definition of *basic*—and the expectations attached to it—has been raised for reading and writing, so, too, has it been raised for mathematics. High schools across the country are raising the minimum number of years that students must study mathematics in order to earn a high school diploma. And just as ability groupings are being dropped in the language arts, so are they being dropped in mathematics. No more "easy" math; no more one year and you're done.

Mathematics through tenth-grade algebra and geometry is becoming the minimum standard. The following overview of just 12 states suggests the consistency of expectations that are becoming the norm throughout the country.

Remember, the term *exit exam* means an examination which must be passed in order to earn a high school diploma.

**CALIFORNIA    HSEE (High School Exit Exam)     2004 exit exam**

Math skills through grade ten Algebra 1 will be tested. You'll find the following areas targeted:

1. Statistics
2. Data analysis and probability
3. Number sense
4. Measurement and geometry
5. Mathematical reasoning
6. Algebra (no quadratic equations)

- No calculator use
- No formulas provided other than for conversions between systems
- 80 multiple-choice; 12 Algebra 1 problems with no quadratic equations
- All multiple-choice

**FLORIDA    FCAT (Florida Comprehensive Assessment Test)     current exit exam**

Note: This test is administered as an exit requirement for grade nine students entering in 1999 and after.

(math skills through grade ten Algebra 1)

1. Number sense, concepts, operations
2. Measurement
3. Geometry and spatial sense
4. Algebraic thinking
5. Data analysis and probability

**GEORGIA    GHSGT (Georgia High School Graduation Test)     current exit exam**

(math skills through grade ten Algebra 1)

1. Numbers and computation
2. Data analysis
3. Measurement and geometry
4. Algebra
5. All multiple-choice

**NORTH CAROLINA     NCHSEE (North Carolina High School Exit Exam)     2003 exit exam**

Note: This test is administered for the first time to eleventh graders in Spring 2002 as an exit requirement.

(math skills through grade ten Algebra 1)

1. Real number operations and relationships
2. Geometry and spatial sense
3. Algebraic concepts to make predictions
4. Data analysis and probability
5. Mathematical reasoning (relationships between fractions/decimals/percents)

▶ Calculator use
▶ Formulas and tables provided
▶ 60–80 multiple-choice items
▶ All multiple-choice
▶ Questions will require solving specific problems from work and home.

**NEW YORK     NYSRE MATH A (New York State Regents Exam Math A)     2004–2005 exit exam**

Note: This test is an exit requirement for students entering grade nine in 2001 and after.

(math skills through grade ten Algebra 1)

1. Mathematical reasoning
2. Numbers and numeration
3. Operations and relationships
4. Geometry and spatial sense
5. Measurement
6. Probability and statistics
7. Algebraic concepts
8. Quadratic equations

▶ Scientific calculators required
▶ Graphing calculators allowed but not required
▶ Straightedge and compass required
▶ 15 performance task items; 20 multiple-choice items
▶ Multiple-choice and performance task items with applications to real-world situations

**OHIO      HSGQE (High School Graduation Qualifying Exam)      current exit exam**

(math skills through grade ten Algebra 1)

1. Numbers and numeracy
2. Algebra and functions
3. Geometry and measurement
4. Data analysis and probability
5. Mathematical processes

▶ Scientific calculator allowed
▶ 50 items; 44 multiple-choice; 4 short answer; 2 extended response
▶ Multiple-choice, short answer and extended response questions will be drawn from real-world contexts.


**TEXAS      TAKS (Texas Assessment of Knowledge and Skills)      current exit exam**

(math skills through grade ten Algebra)

1. Number concepts
2. Algebraic/mathematical relationships and functions
3. Geometric properties and relationships
4. Measurement concepts
5. Probability and statistics
6. Addition/multiplication/division/subtraction to solve problems
7. Problem solving using estimation
8. Problem solving using solution strategies
9. Problem solving using mathematical representation
10. Evaluation of the reasonableness of a solution

▶ 60 multiple-choice items


**PENNSYLVANIA      PSSA (Pennsylvania Student Skills Assessment)      not yet an exit exam**

(math skills through grade eleven)

1. Numbers, number systems, number relationships
2. Computation and estimation
3. Measurement and estimation
4. Mathematical reasoning and connections
5. Mathematical problem solving and communication
6. Statistics and data analysis
7. Probability and predictions
8. Algebra and functions

9. Geometry

10. Trigonometry

11. Concepts of calculus

▶ 15 points open-ended. "Open-ended tasks present real-life situations that require students to solve a problem using math abilities learned in the classroom; students must provide a written solution."

▶ 85 points multiple-choice


**MARYLAND    MHSA (Maryland High School Assessment)    current end of course exam; not an exit exam until 2007**

(math skills through grade ten Algebra 1)

1. Functions and algebra

2. Geometry, measurement, and reasoning

3. Data analysis and probability

4. Conceptual understandings

5. Multiple representations and connections

6. Mathematical modeling

7. Mathematical problem solving

▶ "Single response, brief constructed response, and extended constructed response items will require students to solve real-world problems with graphic representation playing an important role."


**DELAWARE    DSTP (Delaware Student Testing Program)    current exit exam**

(math skills through grade ten Algebra 1)

1. Solve problems

2. Communicate mathematically

3. Reason mathematically

4. Make mathematical connections

5. Estimation, measurement, and computation

6. Number sense

7. Algebra (equations, graphs)

8. Geometry and spatial sense

9. Statistics and probability

10. Patterns, relationships and functions

▶ Calculator use allowed

▶ Multiple-choice, short answer, and extended response

**CONNECTICUT    CAPT II (Connecticut Academic Performance Test)    not an exit exam**

(math skills through grade ten Algebra 1)

1.  Number sense
2.  Operations
3.  Estimation and approximation
4.  Ratios, proportions, and percents
5.  Measurement
6.  Spatial relationships and geometry
7.  Probability and statistics
8.  Patterns
9.  Algebra and functions
10.  Discrete mathematics

▶ 8 open-ended items; 24 grid-in items

▶ Calculator use allowed

▶ Students will compute, estimate, and solve problems from real-world scenarios with open-ended and constructed response questions.

**NEW JERSEY    HSPA (High School Proficiency Assessment)
replaces HSPT in 2002    current exit exam**

(math skills through Algebra 1 including Trigonometry and pre-Calculus)

1.  Number sense and concepts
2.  Spatial sense and geometry
3.  Data analysis, probability, statistics, and discrete mathematics
4.  Patterns and functions of Algebra

▶ Calculator use allowed

▶ 26–31 multiple-choice items; 7 open-ended items; 4 short constructed response items

### *Common Themes*

Notice the common themes: math through grade ten, including algebra and geometry; a combination of multiple-choice and constructed response questions; and "real-world" applications. For our purposes in this book, we can summarize the math skills being tested into four categories with sub-topics:

1. **Number Sense and Concepts**
   - Operations with rational and irrational numbers
   - Percents
   - Proportions and ratios
   - Scientific notation
   - Powers and roots

2. **Spatial Sense and Geometry**
   - Calculating perimeters, areas, surface areas, and volumes of common plane figures and 3-D solids
   - Pythagorean Theorem
   - Similar figures
   - Right triangle trigonometry
   - Estimation strategies
   - Transformations
   - Coordinate geometry

3. **Data Analysis, Probability and Statistics, and Discrete Mathematics**
   - Theoretical and experimental probability
   - Compound events (dependent and independent)
   - Mean, median, and mode
   - Graphing data (circle graphs, bar graphs, histograms, tables, stem-and-leaf plots)
   - Combinations
   - Permutations

4. **Patterns, Functions, and Algebra**
   - Arithmetic and geometric series
   - Number patterns
   - Linear functions
   - Creating and manipulating algebraic equations

Now let's see how you actually test a student's ability to do all that!

**NUMBER SENSE AND CONCEPTS**

1. Of the numbers listed, which choice is not equivalent to the others?
   a. .034%
   b. $3.4 \times 10^{-4}$
   c. $\frac{34}{100,000}$
   d. .0034

The correct answer is choice **d**. By converting each of the choices given in the question we can easily eliminate the choice that is not equivalent. Choice **a** is given in percentage form, which is equivalent to dividing by 100: .034% = $\frac{.034}{100}$ = .00034. Choice **b** is given in scientific notation. When the exponent or the power of ten is negative the number represented is a small number. You can convert the coefficient of the choice given in scientific notation, 3.4, to a decimal by moving the decimal four places to the left, $3.4 \times 10^{-4}$ = .00034. Choice **c** is given in fractional form which when converted to a decimal is .00034. Clearly choice **d**, already given in decimal form, is not equivalent to the first three choices.

Question 1 tests several number concepts, including converting percents to decimal equivalents, converting percents to fractional equivalents, and scientific notation.

2. What is 30% of 20% of 38,000?
    a. 1900
    b. 2280
    c. 2400
    d. 3800

The correct answer is choice **b**. 30% of 20% of 38,000 can be written mathematically as $.30 \times .20 \times 38{,}000$, which equals 2280.

Question 2 is an example of how a student's knowledge of operations with percents might be tested.

3. What type of number solves the equation $x^2 = 2$?
    a. a rational number
    b. an integer
    c. an irrational number
    d. a prime number

The correct answer is **c**. If $x^2 = 2$, then $\sqrt{x^2} = \sqrt{2}$, and $x = \sqrt{2}$. The variable $x$ would therefore be an irrational number because it cannot be expressed as a ratio of 2 integers. Integers = { . . . , $-3, -2, -2, 0, 1, 2, 3, \ldots$ }. Rational numbers can be expressed as the ratio of 2 integers, such as $\frac{6}{5}$ or $\frac{12}{3}$. Prime numbers have only 2 positive factors: 1 and the number itself. The factors of a prime number must be integers.

Question 3 tests number terminology and an application of number concepts.
    ▶ Rational numbers
    ▶ Irrational numbers

- ▶ Prime numbers
- ▶ Integers
- ▶ Whole numbers
- ▶ Real numbers

4. (Short Answer) Find the quotient of $11.5 \times 10^{11} \div 2.3 \times 10^8$. Express your answer in scientific notation. Show all work.

$$\frac{11.5 \times 10^{11}}{2.3 \times 10^8} = \frac{11.5 \times 10^3}{2.3} =$$

The correct answer is $5.0 \times 10^3$.

Question 4 tests a student's ability to manipulate values represented in scientific notation. Note that to be successful, the student must be able to apply the rules for performing operations on exponents. When dividing powers of ten (scientific notation), subtract the exponents. Therefore, $10^{11} \div 10^8 = 10^3$. The coefficients are divided normally.

### SPATIAL SENSE AND GEOMETRY

1. Which equation can be used to find the height, $h$, of the telephone pole?

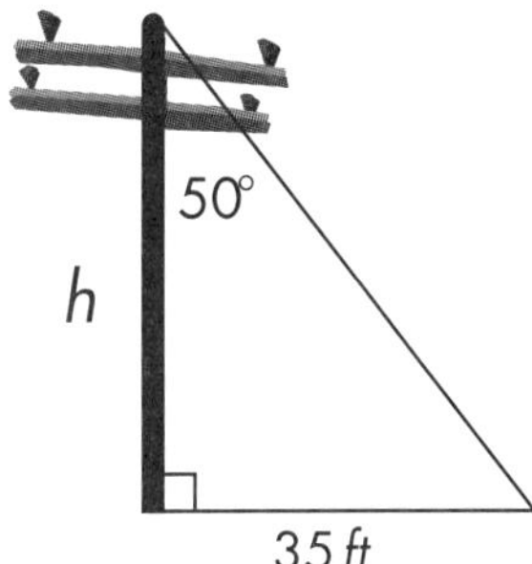


   **a.** $\sin 50 = \frac{h}{35}$

   **b.** $\tan 50 = \frac{35}{h}$

   **c.** $\cos 50 = \frac{h}{35}$

   **d.** $\tan 50 = \frac{h}{35}$

The correct answer is **b.** In order to find $h$, you should use the ratio of the side opposite the 50° to the side adjacent to the 50°. $\tan \theta = \frac{\text{opp}}{\text{adj}}$, so $\tan 50 = \frac{35}{h}$.

Question 1 tests the student's ability to use the trigonometric ratios in a "real-world" setting.

**2.**

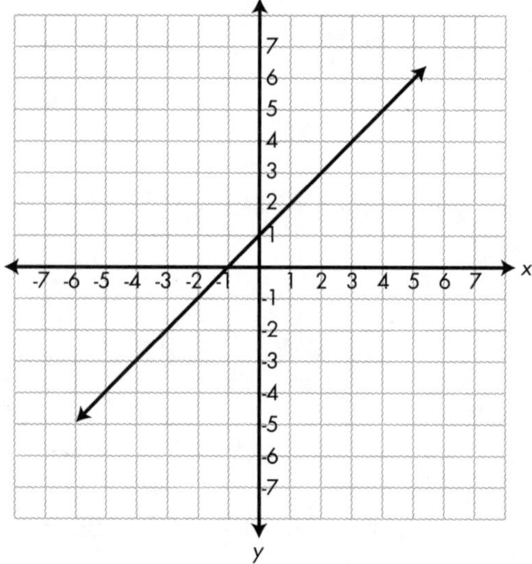

Which table of coordinates is represented by the graph above?

**a.**

| x | y |
|---|---|
| 4 | 5 |
| 1 | 0 |
| 2 | 3 |
| 5 | 4 |

**c.**

| x | y |
|---|---|
| −5 | 4 |
| −1 | 0 |
| 2 | 3 |
| 4 | 5 |

**b.**

| x | y |
|---|---|
| 4 | −5 |
| −1 | 0 |
| 3 | 2 |
| 5 | 4 |

**d.**

| x | y |
|---|---|
| −4 | −5 |
| −1 | 0 |
| 2 | −3 |
| 5 | −4 |

The correct answer is **c.** The *x* values are the horizontal values and the *y* values are the vertical values. Keeping this in mind, if you compare the values of each table to the points on the grid, choice **c** is the correct answer.

Question 2 tests a student's ability to compare data to a graphical representation of a line on the coordinate plane.

3.  When the label of the can below is peeled off, what is its area? Assume that there
    is no overlapping of the edges of the label.

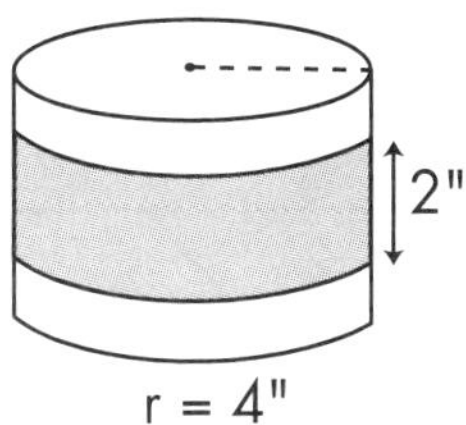


Use the formula C = $\pi d$ to solve for the circumference of the cylinder. C = $\pi d$ = $8\pi$.
Notice that the circumference of the cylinder is actually the length of the rectangular
label. The width of the label is 2″. To find the area of this label, simply use A = L × W
= $8\pi$ × 2″ = $16\pi$ inches.

Question 3 measures geometry skills.

4.  The volume of a cube is 343 cm$^3$.

    **Part A:** Find the surface area of this cube.

    **Part B:** Suppose that 8 such cubes are combined into a large cube. Find the ratio
    of the surface area of the initial cube to the volume of this new large cube. Show
    all work.
    Answer: Note: V = volume, $s$ = side, SA = surface area.
    **Part A:**

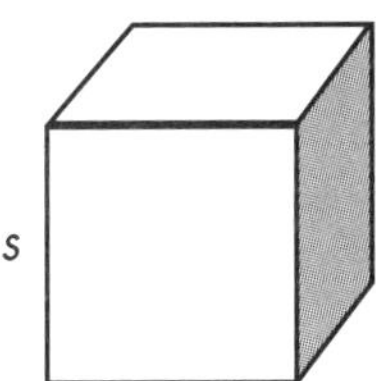


Volume = $s^3$

V = $s^3$

V = 343 cm$^3$

V = $7^3$

$s^3 = 7^3$

$s$ = 7

The area of each face = 7 × 7 = 49 cm². A cube has six faces, so the surface area would
be 6 × 49 = 294 cm².

(Alternatively, a student may use the surface area formula for a cube: S.A. = $6s^2$.)

Eight such cubes would be arranged into a larger cube by arranging four cubes into a square to form a bottom layer and placing four more cubes on top to form a top layer.

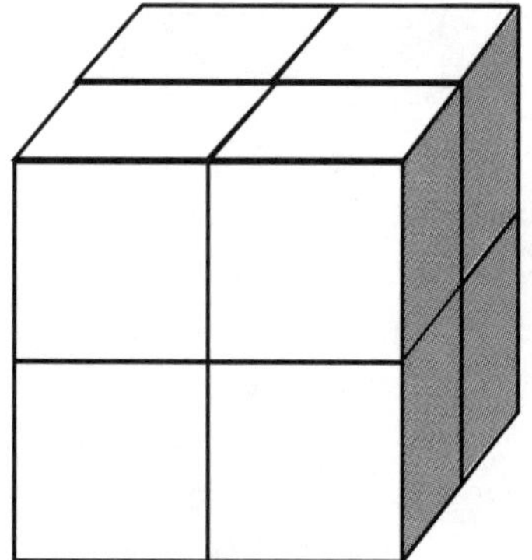

The side of each face would then be 14 (2 times the original side of 7), and the area of each face would be $A = s^2 = 14^2 = 196$ cm$^2$. A cube has 6 faces, so the surface area of this larger cube would be $196 \times 6 = 1176$ cm$^2$. 1176 cm$^2$ is four times the surface area of the smaller cube. (This is because $1176 \div 294 = 4$). The ratio of the S.A. of the initial cube to the larger cube is then 1:4.

Question 4 measures geometry skills.

### DATA ANALYSIS, PROBABILITY AND STATISTICS, AND DISCRETE MATHEMATICS

1. Mr. Cohen used a stem-and-leaf plot to chart the outcome of his final exam. What was the mode of this exam?

| Stem | Leaves |
|------|--------|
| 6 | 0 1 8 |
| 7 | 2 2 5 |
| 8 | 0 3 3 3 6 |
| 9 | 2 5 6 7 |

Key: 7 | 2 = 72

   a. 3
   b. 72
   c. 83
   d. 95

The correct answer is **c**. Here you must use the key to see that the "stem" is the tenths place of the score and the "leaves" are the ones place. The mode would be the test score that occurs most. Here, the stem of 8 and the leaf of 3 occurs most. Thus, the mode is 83.

Question 1 tests a student's ability to interpret a stem-and-leaf plot. It also incorporates the concept of mode.

2. Martin makes $\$x$ an hour. If his rate of pay does not change, which graph below could represent a plot of dollars earned verses hours worked?

**a.**

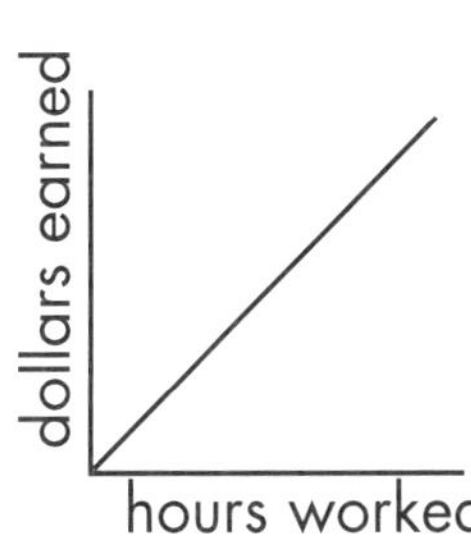


**c.**

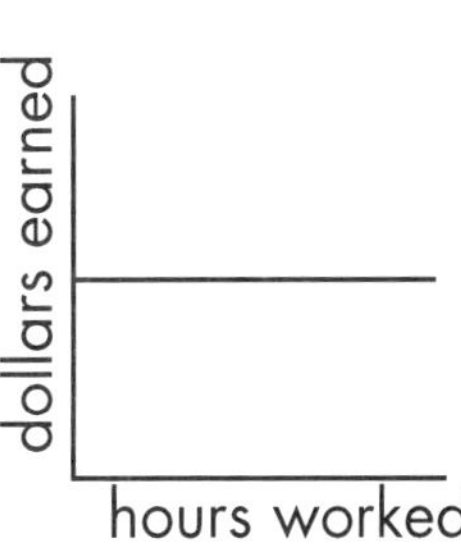


**b.**

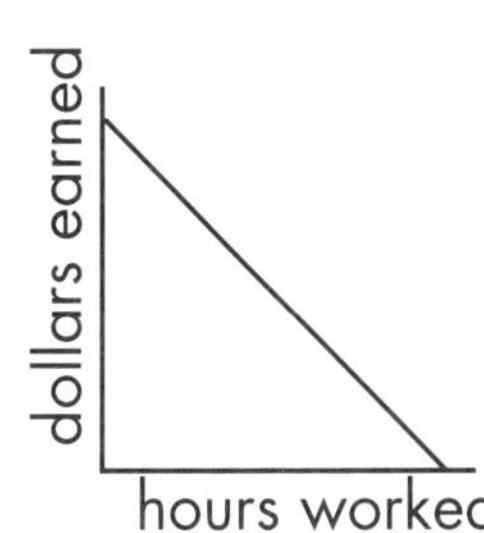


**d.**

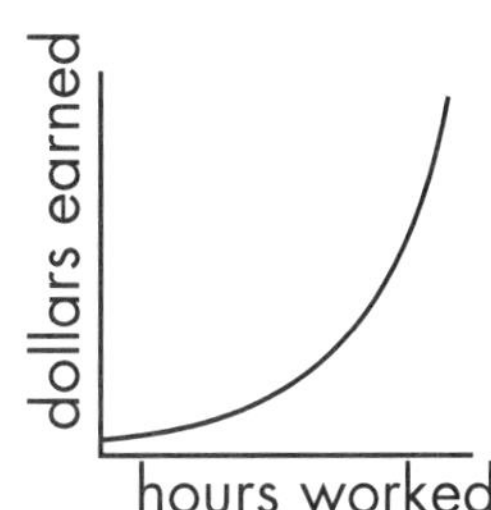


The correct answer is **a**. If Martin works 0 hours, he will make 0 dollars. The $(x,y)$ coordinates that correspond to this statement are $(0,0)$. The more hours he works, the more money he makes. His earnings are directly proportional to the amount of hours he puts in. Choice **a** represents a direct increase in earnings as hours increase.

Question 2 tests a student's ability to graphically represent "real-world" information. At the high school level, students should be able to recognize the following types of relationships:

▶ Direct Relationships
▶ Inverse Relationships
▶ Exponential Relationships

3.  If 9 students out of 16 will be randomly chosen to participate in a trivia contest, how many combinations are possible?

a.  57,657,600

b.  144,110

c.  11,440

d.  144

The correct answer is **c.** Here we use the combination formula for $n$ elements $r$ at a time:

$$n! \div (n-r)!r! = 16! \div (16-9)!9! = 16! \div (7)!9!$$

$$= 16 \times 15 \times 14 \times 13 \times 12 \times 11 \times 10 \times 9 \times 8 \times 7 \times 6 \times 5 \times 4 \times 3 \times 2 \times 1$$

$$\div (7 \times 6 \times 5 \times 4 \times 3 \times 2 \times 1)(9 \times 8 \times 7 \times 6 \times 5 \times 4 \times 3 \times 2 \times 1 \times) =$$

$$\frac{16 \times 15 \times 14 \times 13 \times 12 \times 11 \times 10}{7 \times 6 \times 5 \times 4 \times 3 \times 2 \times 1} = 57,657,600 \div 5,040 = 11,440$$

$n!$ = "$n$ factorial." For example, $4! = 4 \times 3 \times 2 \times 1$.

Question 3 presents a "real-world" instance where an application of the combination formula would be used. Students at the high school level should know how to discern when to use the permutation formula versus when to use the combination formula. Usually a reference sheet with these 2 formulas are provided for the student who is taking the exit exam. Sometimes students rely on their high tech calculator to instantly perform these calculations. Although some states allow calculators on examinations, they usually <u>do not</u> allow students to use their own high tech calculators! Therefore, a student would be wise to practice these calculations without the aid of a high tech calculator.

4.  The spinner below is fair. It will be spun twice and the results will be recorded.

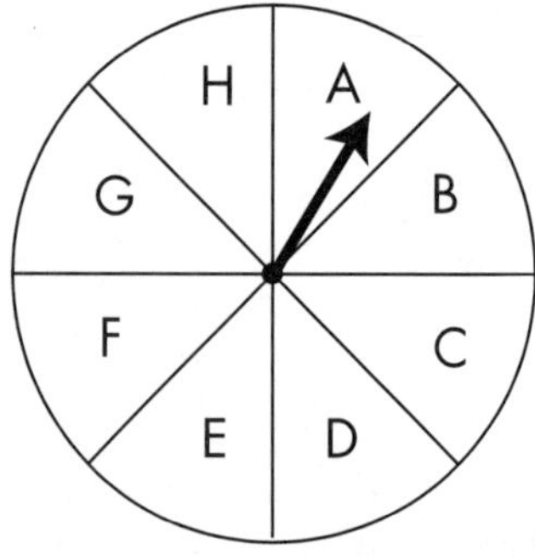


**Part A:** What is the probability that the spinner will land on A for spin 1 and B for spin 2?

**Part B:** What is the probability the spinner will land on B or C during either of the spins?

**Part A:** (A <u>and</u> B means *multiply* both probabilities)

$\frac{1}{8} \times \frac{1}{8} = \frac{1}{64}$

**Part B:** Probability of B or C (B <u>or</u> C means *add* both probabilities):

$\frac{1}{8} + \frac{1}{8} = \frac{2}{8}$ or $\frac{1}{4}$ each time it is spun.

Probability of successful outcome for Spin 1 or Spin 2 (Spin 1 <u>or</u> Spin 2 means *add* both probabilities):

$\frac{1}{4} + \frac{1}{4} = \frac{1}{2}$

Question 4 addresses calculating probabilities. At the high school level, students should be able to determine probabilities of independent and dependent events.

### PATTERNS, FUNCTIONS, AND ALGEBRA

1. What is the fifth term in the series below?

    $3x^2, 9x^3, 27x^4, \ldots$
    a. $36x^5$
    b. $45x^5$
    c. $81x^5$
    d. $243x^6$

The correct answer is **d.** The coefficient of each term is 3 times the coefficient of the preceding term. The power of each variable is one more than the power of the variable in the term prior. The fourth term would then be $81x^5$ and the fifth term is $243x^6$. Each successive term can be found by multiplying the preceding term by $3x$.

Question 1 deals with patterns and series. At the high school level, students should be able to recognize arithmetic series, geometric series, and discern the pattern for series that are neither arithmetic or geometric.

2. What is the sum of $2x^2 + 3x - 1$ and $x^2 + 5x - 5$?
    a. $3x^2 + 8x - 4$
    b. $3x^2 + 2x + 4$
    c. $3x^2 + 8x - 6$
    d. $3x^2 + 8x + 6$

The correct answer is **c.** Use a simultaneous equation to add the two given equations:

$$2x^2 + 3x - 1$$
$$\underline{+ (x^2 + 5x - 5)}$$
$$3x^2 + 8x - 6$$

Question 2 requires the student to know how to add algebraic expressions. At the high school level, students should be able to use simultaneous equations to quickly combine algebraic equations. However, this question could have been solved without simultaneous equations, for example, by combining like terms.

3. $\frac{y^2 + 5y}{y}$ is equivalent to
   a. $y + 5y$
   b. $y + 5$
   c. $y^2 + 5$
   d. $y(y + 5)$

The correct answer is **b.** Factoring the numerator yields $\frac{y(y + 5)}{y}$. The $y$ in the numerator cancels with the $y$ in the denominator, yielding $y + 5$.

Question 3 requires the student to simplify an expression via factoring.

4. If $D = kx + \frac{2}{L}$, what does L equal?
   Answer:
   $$D = kx + \frac{2}{L}$$
   $$D - kx = \frac{2}{L}$$
   $$L(D - kx) = 2$$
   $$L = \frac{2}{D - kx}$$

Remember, when you isolate a variable or manipulate an algebraic equation, you must perform each step on **both** sides of the equation.

Question 4 is a Show Your Work question. It requires a student to be able to manipulate an equation in order to isolate a variable. It is also not a multiple-choice question but one which requires that a student demonstrate how the answer was derived.

Some states go even further than grade 10 math and include trigonometry and even pre-calculus on their exams. To determine exactly what your state requires, you must access the state website or speak to your child's math teacher, building principal, or district office curriculum coordinator.

# Looking at Middle School Exams: English/ Language Arts

**As mentioned** earlier, the middle school examinations in English/Language Arts and mathematics are indicators of a student's progress towards the important high school diploma requirement. It is not surprising then, that the grade eight test instrument looks very much like the grade ten or eleven test instrument, because both tests have been carefully aligned with the state's standards that we talked about in Chapters 1 and 2.

# Teaching to the Test

THE CONSISTENCY OF the test formats between middle and high school also enables teachers to develop instructional practices that will prepare students for the tests. Some interpret this as "teaching to the test." Teachers, parents, and school district administrators all across the United States are very concerned that in fourth grade and eighth grade almost the entire month of May or June can be given over to testing. Many are also concerned that in addition to the actual testing time, valuable classroom instructional time is spent drilling children on how to take the test(s). But good tests can also promote good teaching. That is why the tests must be aligned with the content standards and why test items must represent performance indicators for those standards.

Let's go back to the "Miss Brill" short story in Chapter 3. Good instructional practice in a high school English classroom will find students reading such works of literature and answering questions, which probe both literal and inferential levels of comprehension. Students will read lots of literature this way and not just for test preparation but because it's a good way to read a lot and discuss literary issues frequently. In short, it's good English teaching.

Similarly, a good English classroom—whether it's high school, junior high, or middle school—will find students writing often, for a variety of purposes including responses to literature, persuasion, narration, and exposition. English teachers familiar with current research about writing know that students need to write and receive feedback on the quality of their efforts. So, too, students need to be familiar with the criteria charts that are being used to evaluate them and their writing should receive constant feedback applying that criteria.

There should be no surprises, then, on a state test at any level because the state standards should have been used to develop curriculum materials, which drive instructional practices, and most of the new state tests have been carefully aligned with their state's standards.

So let's look at the middle or junior high school assessment in English/Language Arts. This test is generally administered in grade eight, in some states in grade six, and it will measure reading, writing, listening, and speaking in much the same way that the high school test does. The reading passages will be shorter and more age and grade appropriate, but the emphasis will be similar. Reading for literal and inferential comprehension, writing to narrate, persuade, or explain—either in response to text (text-based) or stand-alone prompts—continues to be the theme here.

For example, in Florida, the state (Florida Comprehensive Assessment Test—FCAT) has two writing prompts for grade eight. One asks students to explain why a particular day is special and the other to persuade a teacher to visit a particular place on a field trip.

In reading, Florida has students construct meaning (multiple-choice and open-ended responses) from informational text and from literature.

In Delaware (Delaware Student Testing Program—DSTP), students must read literature and informational and technical documents, and answer multiple-choice questions, short answer questions, and extended response questions to demonstrate their ability to analyze and interpret what they have read. They must also write in response to a stand-alone prompt and then "to reflect that reading and writing are integrally connected, students are asked to write a short essay responding to a question about a reading passage."

In Texas (Texas Assessment of Knowledge and Skills—TAKS) students in grade eight will demonstrate reading and writing proficiency when reading and responding to multiple-choice and extended writing including tasks. These tasks ask that students read two comparable pieces and use information gleaned from both in a response.

In New York, grade eight students will listen to a passage and answer multiple-choice/written response questions related to the passage. They will read two related passages and write three short and one full-length response. Last, they will write a full-length (stand-alone) composition.

The list is similar in all 50 states. So let's look at typical grade eight reading comprehension questions based on *informational* text.


## Knoxville Leads the Nation in Success with Red Pandas

*By Amy McRary*

The Knoxville Zoo has earned a stellar reputation in the past twenty years for its work with endangered red pandas.

Red pandas are sometimes called the lesser panda because of their larger, more well known relative, the giant panda. Curious animals with thick orange-red fur and ringed tails, red pandas look like a cross between a raccoon and a fox. Since the animals are about the size of a raccoon, a medium-sized zoo like Knoxville can exhibit several pairs. "It's harder to learn a lot about an animal if you only have one or two individuals," says Greta McMillan, Animal Collections Coordinator.

No one is sure how many of the bamboo-eating animals remain in the wild. The World Wildlife Fund has designated their native Himalayans as one of the world's most endangered habitats.

The Knoxville Zoo's first pair of pandas, named Buster and Beatrice, arrived in 1977 on a breeding loan from the National Zoo in Washington. Their first cubs were born in 1978 and started a summer birthing trend.

Fifty-six red pandas have been born at the Knoxville Zoo, the most born at any North American zoo and second most in the world. The Netherlands' Rotterdam Zoo is first worldwide, with just more than 60 births. Red pandas typically have two cubs in a litter.

The lives of captive red pandas were systematically managed for a decade before the American Zoo and Aquarium Association established a formal Species Survival Plan in 1985. Then 76 pandas lived in 26 U. S. zoos. Today, 172 animals live in 52 parks.

The Knoxville Zoo now has three pairs of breeding-age red pandas and four young cubs. In 1995, the zoo received one of three red pandas from the zoo in Madrid, Spain. Silvia, a mother who has had two litters since arriving in Knoxville, represents a new bloodline. Because the Spanish pandas weren't related to any American animals, they enlarged the species' gene pool. Silvia also is panda royalty, descended from the last red pandas legally taken from their native land. The king of Nepal gave Silvia's ancestors to Spain's king in the 1980s.

The zoo's success with red pandas can be attributed to "good care and attention," says the Miles Roberts, the longtime Species Survival Plan coordinator for red pandas at National Zoo. "The Knoxville Zoo by no means has the best facilities, but the thing that has made them successful with red pandas is that they treated them as a "star" species and as one of the most important species they could have at the zoo."

The Knoxville Zoo developed a hands-on approach in caring for red pandas, a style it has taught other zoos. That approach has helped reduce infant panda mortality, says Greta McMillan.

The zoo's method blends practical considerations with scientific knowledge. Tennessee's climate is similar to the pandas' native habitat, so their food staple of bamboo can be grown here.

Then there's the method of panda care. Knoxville's animals are habituated enough to humans that keepers can part an animal's thick fur to check its skin. It can take a year to accustom an adult animal to keeper, but McMillan stresses the pandas aren't pets. "The only contact we have with them is contact that is necessary for their survival."

Contact with a new adult panda begins with keepers sitting inside the animal's enclosure for about an hour a day. Later the keeper stands near the panda while the animal eats. Through gradual steps over days, or weeks, keepers place a hand on the animal. "After a point, they learn to trust your proximity," McMillan says.

    **A PARENT'S GUIDE TO HIGH STAKES TESTING**

The technique is increasingly important when 100-gram panda cubs are born. Red pandas don't appear out of their next box until they are about three-and-a-half months old. The challenge is to ensure they are healthy in their first months. Because the animals are accustomed to them, keepers can shift the mother panda to check the cubs.

Babies are checked by keepers the day they are born and then again the next day. The zoo then weighs the animals weekly unless they need further medical attention. "We have to know if they are eating, gaining weight," McMillan says. "The goal is really to let the mom rear them."

So if you want to see red pandas, the Knoxville Zoo in Knoxville, Tennessee is the place to go.

*Reprinted by permission from the Knoxville News-Sentinel.*

### MULTIPLE-CHOICE QUESTIONS

(The specific reading skill that is being tested is listed after each of the four choices.)

1.  The main idea of this article is that
    a.  the Knoxville Zoo is a major tourist attraction.
    b.  the red panda is soon to be extinct.
    c.  the Knoxville Zoo has developed techniques to help the red panda survive.
    d.  the red panda eats bamboo.

The correct answer is **c.** Choices **a** and **d** are mentioned in the article, but they are isolated pieces of information, not the main idea. Choice **b** is incorrect and is not included in the article. Only choice **c** represents the main idea.

The skill tested in this question is recognition of the central idea.

2.  In paragraph 10, the word *habituated* means:
    a.  The red pandas are happy at the zoo.
    b.  The red pandas have accepted the zoo as if it were their natural habitat.
    c.  The zookeepers are having fun with the animals.
    d.  The red pandas and the zookeepers understand each other.

The correct answer is choice **b.** Choices **a, c,** and **d** can be inferred from the article, but only choice **b** defines the word *habituated.*

The skill tested in this question is identifying vocabulary in context.

3. It can be concluded from this article that the Knoxville Zoo
    a. has the best zoo facilities in the nation.
    b. has the most skilled animal keepers in the nation.
    c. provides lots of attention and good care to the red pandas.
    d. attracts endangered species to its collection.

The correct answer is **c**. Paragraph seven says that the Knoxville Zoo *does not* have the best facilities. Nowhere in the article does it say that the most skilled animal keepers in the nation are there (**b**) or that the Knoxville Zoo attracts endangered species to its collection (choice **d**). However, in paragraph seven it clearly states that "good care and attention" are what distinguishes the Knoxville Zoo's success with the red pandas.

The skill tested in the question is drawing conclusions from the text.

4. According to the article, why is it important for keepers to be able to put their hands on the adult red pandas?
    a. The pandas need to be cleaned regularly.
    b. The pandas are dangerous unless they like their keepers.
    c. The pandas must be trained for tourists to pet them.
    d. When new cubs are born, the keepers must check them by lifting the mothers.

The correct answer is **d**. Choices **a**, **b**, and **c** are not stated in the article. Paragraph 12 states that the importance for handling the pandas is to check on newborn cubs.

The skill tested in this question is recognition of supporting details.

5. According to the article, the primary purpose of the Knoxville Zoo's red panda program is to
    a. provide a home for red pandas that no one wants.
    b. develop a major tourist attraction for Tennessee.
    c. promote the future of an endangered species.
    d. promote the red panda as a national symbol.

The correct choice is **c**. Even though paragraphs four, five, and six talk about cubs coming from other places, nowhere is it suggested that it was because they were unwanted; therefore, choice **a** is incorrect. Choices **b** and **d** are also not mentioned in the article.

The skill tested in this question is the ability to paraphrase or retell.

**6.** A reason that the Knoxville Zoo is successful with red pandas is that
   **a.** East Tennessee's climate is similar to the pandas' native habitat.
   **b.** the bamboo that red pandas eat grows wild in East Tennessee.
   **c.** the red pandas have a larger area in which to roam free in East Tennessee.
   **d.** the red pandas get better care and attention at the Knoxville Zoo than anywhere else.

The correct answer is choice **a.** Choice **b** is incorrect. Bamboo does not grow wild in East Tennessee, but it can be grown because of the climate. Choices **c** and **d** are not stated in the article.

The skill tested in this question is recognition of supporting details

**7.** Since 1985 and the Species Survival Plan
   **a.** more red pandas live in fewer parks (zoos).
   **b.** fewer pandas live in more parks (zoos).
   **c.** more pandas live in more parks (zoos).
   **d.** fewer pandas live in fewer parks (zoos).

According to paragraph five, choice **c** is correct.

The skill tested in this question is the ability to extrapolate information.

**8.** What was important about the introduction of Silvia to the red pandas at the Knoxville Zoo?
   **a.** She introduced a new color to the animals.
   **b.** She came from Spain.
   **c.** She introduced a new gene pool.
   **d.** She was the largest of the pandas ever to come to the zoo.

The correct choice is **c.** Paragraph six gives details about Silvia, but the most important point is that Silvia introduced a new gene pool to the species.

The skill tested in this question is the ability to paraphrase or retell.

**9.** How many panda cubs are usually born to a mother?
   **a.** three
   **b.** four
   **c.** two
   **d.** one

The correct choice is **c.** Paragraph four gives this answer.

The skill tested in this question is recognition of supporting details.

**10.** A purpose for reading this article would be to

  **a.** gather information about red pandas.

  **b.** promote people to visit the Knoxville Zoo.

  **c.** persuade Congress to pass laws to protect the red pandas.

  **d.** help train keepers to deal with red pandas.

The correct answer is **a.** People may want to visit the zoo (**b**) and they may even want to persuade Congress for money to protect the red pandas (**c**), but nowhere in the article is that stated or encouraged. Similarly, it can be inferred from the article that Knoxville zookeepers should be emulated (**d**) but the purpose for reading is simply to learn information about the red pandas at the Knoxville Zoo.

This question tests the ability to recognize the purpose of reading this article.

Now let's take a look at a question based on *literary* text. Like the reading for information above, this reading is shorter than the high school reading.

## *The Path Through The Cemetery*
### *By Leonard Q. Ross*

Ivan was a timid little man—so timid that the villagers called him "Pigeon" or mocked him with the title, "Ivan the Terrible." Every night Ivan stopped in at the saloon that was on the edge of the village cemetery. Ivan never crossed the cemetery to get to his lonely shack on the other side. That path would save many minutes but he had never taken it—not even in the full light of noon.

Late one winter's night, when bitter wind and snow beat against the saloon, the customers took up the familiar mockery. "Ivan's mother was scared by a canary when she carried him." "Ivan the terrible—Ivan the Terribly Timid One."

Ivan's sickly protest only fed their taunts, and they jeered cruelly when the young Cossack Lieutenant flung his horrid challenge at their quarry.

"You are a pigeon, Ivan. You'll walk all around the cemetery in this cold—but you dare not cross it."

Ivan murmured, "The cemetery is nothing to cross, Lieutenant. It is nothing but earth, like all the other earth."

The Lieutenant cried, "A challenge, then! Cross the cemetery tonight, Ivan, and I'll give you five rubles—five gold rubles!"

Perhaps it was the vodka. Perhaps it was the temptation of the five gold rubles. No one ever knew why Ivan, moistening his lips, said suddenly: "Yes, Lieutenant, I'll cross the cemetery!"

The saloon echoed with their disbelief. The Lieutenant winked to the men and unbuckled his saber. "Here, Ivan. When you get to the center of the cemetery, in front of the biggest tomb, stick the saber into the ground. In the morning we shall go there. And if the saber is in the ground—five gold rubles to you!"

Ivan took the saber. The men drank a toast: "To Ivan the Terrible!" They roared with laughter.

The wind howled around Ivan as he closed the door of the saloon behind him. The cold was knife-sharp. He buttoned his long coat and crossed the dirt road. He could hear the Lieutenant's voice, louder than the rest, yelling after him, "Five rubles, pigeon. If you live!"

Ivan pushed the cemetery gate open. He walked fast. "Earth, just earth . . . like any other earth." But the darkness was a massive dread. "Five gold rubles . . . " The wind was cruel and the saber was like ice in his hands. Ivan shivered under the long, thick coat and broke into a limping run.

He recognized the large tomb. He must have sobbed—that was the sound that was drowned in the wind. And he kneeled, cold and terrified, and drove the saber through the crust into the hard ground. With all his strength, he pushed it down to the hilt. It was done. The cemetery . . . the challenge . . . five gold rubles.

Ivan started to rise from his knees. But he could not move. Something held him. Something gripped him in an unyielding and implacable hold. Ivan tugged and lurched and pulled—gasping in his panic, shaken by a monstrous fear. But something held Ivan. He cried out in terror, then made senseless gurgling noises.

They found Ivan, next morning, on the ground in front of the tomb that was in the center of the cemetery. He was frozen to death. The look on his face was not that of a frozen man, but of a man killed by some nameless horror. And the Lieutenant's saber was in the ground where Ivan had pounded it—through the dragging folds of his long coat.

*Reprinted with permission from General Media International, Inc.*

1.  What do the villagers call Ivan?
    a.  a canary
    b.  a terrible person
    c.  a pigeon
    d.  a saber-toothed tiger

The correct answer is **c.** In the first sentence of the story it tells us that Ivan was either called "Pigeon" or "Ivan the Terrible." The reference to a canary is made in paragraph two, and it referred to Ivan's mother. He is never called a terrible person and the only mention of a "saber" is to the weapon that the soldiers use.

The skill tested in this question is recognition of supporting details.

2.  Why do the villagers believe that Ivan is a frightened person?
    a.  He refuses to join the army.
    b.  He lives alone.
    c.  He never takes the shortcut to this shack.
    d.  He drinks a lot of vodka with his friends.

The correct answer is **c.** Choice **a** is incorrect because this is never stated or implied in the story. Choice **b** is incorrect because even though Ivan lives alone, nowhere in the story is there any reference made to this as a reason why people see him as frightened. However, Ivan never takes the shortcut to his shack because it cuts through the cemetery, and he is afraid. Even though the opening of the story takes place in a saloon and mention is made of vodka, nowhere does it say that Ivan drinks a lot; therefore choice **d** is incorrect.

The skill tested in this question is recognition of supporting details.

3.  Why does the Lieutenant offer Ivan five gold rubles?
    a.  He wants to challenge Ivan to a race.
    b.  He is trying to get Ivan to join the fun.
    c.  He wants to make fun of Ivan and his fear.
    d.  He wants to win some money.

Choice **c** is the correct answer. Everyone tries to make fun of Ivan by calling him names and teasing him. When the Lieutenant challenges him it is to make public his fear and to show everyone that he is a coward. Choice **a** is not in the story. Choice **b** is incorrect because nowhere in the story does anyone treat Ivan with courtesy or as if they wanted him to be a part of their good time. Choice **d** is incorrect because the wager never says that Ivan has to pay any money if he loses.

The skill tested in this question is extrapolation of information.

4.  Which experience would BEST help you to understand Ivan's dilemma?
    a.  entering a haunted house all alone
    b.  riding a bicycle in the rain
    c.  being called to the principal's office
    d.  stopping to help a stranger

Choice **a** is the most likely answer because Ivan's fear is based on the unknown; he is afraid of ghosts, which is why the cemetery with its dead people frightens him so much. Being afraid of new tasks such as riding a bicycle in the rain, or of threatening situations such as being called to the principal's office may cause fear, but it is not the same kind of fear. Choice **d** is also not likely to cause anyone to be afraid in the same way that Ivan is afraid.

The skill tested in this question is drawing conclusions.

5.  In paragraph 13 the author writes, "Something held him. Something gripped him in an unyielding and implacable hold." What is the meaning of *implacable*?
    a.  easy to remove
    b.  hard to change
    c.  easy to recover from
    d.  difficult to understand

Choice **b** is the correct answer. Ivan found that he was unable to pull his coat free. He struggled to get it loose. He didn't realize that he had driven the sword through his coat and fixed it solidly to the ground. Therefore, *implacable* most likely means *hard to change*. None of the other choices fit the sentence meaning.

The skill tested in this question is paraphrasing and retelling.

6.  In paragraph 11, the author tells us that "the darkness was a massive dread." This means that Ivan was
    a.  brave.
    b.  cowardly.
    c.  terrified.
    d.  cheerful.

Choice **c** is correct. Massive means something huge. Dread means to look forward to something with great apprehension or fear; therefore the expression "massive dread" means "huge fear" or to be "terrified." Choice **a** and **d** are just the opposite. Choice **b** means to be afraid to do something but it does not mean the extreme fear that terrified does.

The skill tested in this question is paraphrasing and retelling.

7. Ivan tells the Lieutenant that, "The cemetery is nothing to cross, Lieutenant. It is nothing but earth, like all other earth." He is probably
   a. trying to show he is not afraid.
   b. trying to show that he has crossed the cemetery before.
   c. trying to get the Lieutenant to make a wager.
   d. trying to win new friends.

Choice **a** is the correct answer. Ivan never says, or implies, that he has ever crossed the cemetery. As a matter of fact, everyone knows that just the opposite is true; therefore choice **b** is incorrect. The Lieutenant is the one to suggest the wager. There is no evidence that Ivan wanted to do this; therefore choice **c** is incorrect. While it is true that Ivan probably wishes that his comrades would treat him nicely and that he could be a friend, nowhere does the story suggest that Ivan will go to the cemetery just to make friends. He accepts the wager because refusing would prove that he is a "pigeon."

The skill tested in this question is prediction of meaning.

8. Which of the following contributes MOST to the suspense of the story?
   a. the Lieutenant's challenge
   b. the darkness of the night and the weather
   c. Ivan's fear of the cemetery
   d. Ivan's nickname, "Pigeon"

The correct answer is **b**. The author creates a setting for the story that emphasizes the gloom and dread. There are numerous references to the weather being "cruel," with cold that was "knife-sharp." The challenge itself, choice **a,** creates the conflict, and Ivan's fear and his nickname contribute to the plot, but it is the setting in a cemetery at night with dreary weather that contributes most to creating the suspense.

The skill tested in this question is forming opinions.

9. Ivan is in greatest danger when he
   a. decides to wait for help.
   b. accepts the Lieutenant's challenge.
   c. doesn't dress warmly enough.
   d. believes that something or someone is holding him down.

Choice **d** is the correct answer. Ivan goes into a complete panic when he can't release his overcoat. The story tells us that he makes "senseless gurgling" sounds which meant that he lost his senses, or became insane with fear. Accepting the Lieutenant's challenge put him in no more real danger than just going out in the cold, but it is Ivan's fear that caused him to act irrationally and not try to help himself. Choice **b** and choice **c** are therefore incorrect. Choice **a** is incorrect because Ivan is so overcome with fear that he makes no rational decisions at all.

The skill tested in this question is drawing conclusions.

10. One of the lessons that we can learn from this story is
    a. never accept a challenge if you are afraid.
    b. ignore bullies who call you names.
    c. being afraid can be more damaging than what you are afraid of.
    d. the weather is always our worst enemy.

The correct answer is **c**. The story is not telling us that we should never accept challenges, choice **a**. Ivan accepted the challenge to try to prove his courage but it was his fear that overcame him in the end. Even though the weather was bad, choice **d**, the story does not state or imply that it was the weather that caused Ivan's death. And choice **b**, though good advice, is not suggested by the story.

The skill tested in this question is prediction of meaning.

**OPEN-ENDED QUESTIONS**

11. Ivan was afraid to cross the cemetery, but he accepted the Lieutenant's challenge.
    ▶ Give two reasons why someone would accept such a challenge.
    ▶ Describe what happened to Ivan.

Use information from the story to support your answers.

12. This story is about being afraid and trying to be brave.
    ▶ What would you have done if you were Ivan?
    ▶ How would you have changed the outcome that befell Ivan?

Use information from the story to support your answers.

**Question 11—Score 0 Response:** *I think Ivan is a jerk for wanting to go out in the snow and he reminds me of the biggest snowstorm of the year. We had six feet and a read about a boy who went out with no shoes on and he froze to death. His mother looked for him and almost couldn't find him he was buried in so much snow and his body was all stiff and blue she cried when she saw him. My mother makes me dress too much in the snow because of that boy. He didn't even live near me.*

**Evaluation:** This response does not answer the question. It has nothing to do with the story other than to compare the cold and Ivan's freezing to death with a personal experience.

**Question 11—Score 1 Response:** *I would accept the challenge to go through a cemetery especially if someone gave me money. Ivan wanted to get money so he went to a cemetery and then got scared cause of the ghosts. This story is like the Blair Witch Project where everybody goes to the woods and looks for witches and ghosts and go through scary houses and stuff life that. I once went to a haunted house at Halloween and one of my friend didn't want to go because he was scared but we made him and he started crying so we let him go out. We didn't make fun of him or call him names.*

**Evaluation:** This is a very weak response because it doesn't answer the question. It does not provide two reasons why people would accept a challenge, and it goes off on a tangent about scary places. The writer has some understanding that Ivan was afraid of ghosts but then goes off on a completely irrelevant side story about his or her friends.

**Question 11—Score 2 Response:** *Ivan took the Lieutenant's challenge because he wanted to be part of the group and he really wanted the five gold rubles. People will do a lot of silly stuff for money and even Ivan, who was really scared, was willing to take a risk for money. He also wanted friends and when you do something scary people like to be your friend.*

*Ivan was a soldier that everybody made fun of and he just got tired of it and decided to prove that he was really not afraid of the cemetery. So he took the challenge but he had an accident in the cemetery and he froze to death. The other people probably felt bad that they made him do it because they probably realized that he was a nice friend after all.*

**Evaluation:** This is a weak response. Even though the author realizes that Ivan was trying to be part of the group, he or she misunderstands his desire for the money. The writer also misunderstands what happened to Ivan in the cemetery. The writer does not understand how very terrified Ivan was and that he died because of the saber being run through his coat.

**Question 11—Score 3 Response:** *Ivan is just like many people. He wanted to be liked and he wanted for people to admire him. Lots of my friends feel the same way and many of them would accept a challenge like Ivan's to prove they are strong or smart or whatever. Ivan's challenge was to do something he was really afraid to do. That makes it even harder. But that makes it even more true. If you just do something that anybody could do then it isn't a real challenge.*

*Two reasons to accept a really scary challenge would be to prove to yourself that you're not scared and to prove it to others. One of the best ways to overcome fear is to face it. I remember once being very afraid to ride the big roller coaster at Great Adventure Park. I was with a group of friends and they were teasing me and calling me a baby. I knew that if I didn't ride that I would never get over that nickname but I also knew that there would be lots more roller coasters to ride. So, with my heart pounding I went on with my friend, Jenny. I screamed and nearly cried but when the ride was over I wanted to go again. I knew then that if ever I was afraid all I had to do was overcome it. If Ivan could have come through his challenge he probably would have walked home through the cemetery every night. But instead his fear got the best of him.*

*And that is what really happened to him. He was scared to death. He thought a ghost had grabbed him but it was really just his overcoat that he jammed with the saber. Poor Ivan. He never proved anything to anybody. He died being afraid.*

**Evaluation:** This response clearly answers the questions and demonstrates good understanding of the story. There is some explanation and opinion used that relate to situations in the story. The writer relates a personal experience to prove his or her point and goes on to connect it to the story.

**Question 11—Score 4 Response:** *Ivan was a man who was tired of being made fun of by his friends and neighbors. Even though he was afraid of the cemetery, he knew that unless he accepted the Lieutenant's challenge he could never prove to them that he really wasn't a "pigeon." I can understand why someone would need to prove that he was brave or strong or even just a good friend. People sometimes make you do things you wouldn't normally do.*

*But another reason that Ivan took the challenge could have been just to have fun. The story says that everyone was surprised. They weren't sure if it was the money or the vodka that made Ivan accept. Sometimes when you're in a crowd and having a good time you do silly things just to be part of the group. Ivan wanted to be part of the group and maybe he thought that accepting the challenge would help him make friends.*

*Unfortunately for Ivan, he accepted the challenge, but he wasn't ready for it. He was so afraid that he stopped thinking about what he was doing. He ran into the cemetery and was in such a rush to bury the sword and run away that he didn't realize that he pushed the sword into his coat. When he couldn't get up to run he thought that a ghost or spirit had grabbed him. He died of just being afraid. Ivan never made friends, or proved he was brave. He just died of being scared.*

**Evaluation:** This response clearly answers the question and demonstrates that the writer understood the story. There are two possible reasons stated for accepting a challenge to prove yourself to others; first, to prove them wrong, and second, to have fun and make friends. The writer then goes on to describe exactly what happened to Ivan. There is clear understanding of the task and the writer uses details from the story to support the answer and extend understanding of the text.

**Question 12—Score 0 Response:** *When I go near a cemetery I never go alone and I always go in the day and I always dress in heavy clothes to be sure it doesn't snow. If I went near a cemetery and it started to snow or rain I would run the other way. Just like in the movie about the kids in the haunted house that ran inside for cover from the rain and they found dead bodies and they couldn't get out. I would never go to a strange house even if it was really cold and snowing.*

**Evaluation:** This response has nothing to do with the question. It is not logically organized and rambles from one idea to the next with no connection to the story.

**Question 12—Score 1 Response:** *I would never want to go to a cemetery and be attacked by ghosts like Ivan. I would have run out of the place where all these people were making fun of me and never gone back. I would never go to a cemetery in the dark, all alone, because just like the ghosts got Ivan they could get me.*

*If I wanted to go I would get friends to go with me and then we could bring bells and whistles to scare away the evil spirits. On Halloween my friends wanted to go to the cemetery after dark but my mother said no way.*

**Evaluation:** This response doesn't answer the question fully and does not complete the requirements of the task. There is only one reference to the story, and it is incorrect. Ivan was not attacked by ghosts. He was being held by the saber.

**Question 12—Score 2 Response:** *Ivan wanted friends. He let people talk him into doing anything just so they would like him. I would never take money to be friends with somebody. Ivan should have asked for more money to make it more worth his risk. I would have gotten twice as much to take so much risk. Then I would have run right home and nobody would have known whether I went to the cemetery or not. I would have their money and they could laugh at me all they wanted.*

**Evaluation:** Although the writer explains what he or she would do differently, this answer shows a confused understanding of the story. Ivan didn't take the challenge for the money and there was no amount of money that would have helped him overcome his fear. Also, the writer says that he or she would have run home, ignoring the fact that he or she could only collect the money if they found the saber at the cemetery. This response is an inconsistent and flawed explanation of the story.

**Question 12—Score 3 Response:** *It is always hard to feel like an outsider. Many people would do almost anything to make friends and stop being made fun of. I think Ivan did what most people would do. He tried to prove that he wasn't the "pigeon" that they were calling him. The Lieutenant challenged him because he thought Ivan would have been so scared that he wouldn't take up the bet. The Lieutenant didn't realize that being made fun of is worse than being scared. I would have done the same thing that Ivan did.*

*I don't know if the outcome would have been different for me. Ivan was so scared that he lost his ability to think straight. If I were that scared it could happen to me, too. Once I was very afraid to go with my friends racing on our mini bikes. I was like Ivan. My friends were teasing me and I was scared but then when I was racing I just hoped and prayed a lot. I felt really good about the whole thing afterwards because I had done something I thought would be awful and it turned out that I proved to myself that I could conquer my fear. But what I did wasn't as scary as what Ivan had to do and none of my friends really knew just how scared I was. Ivan was forced to go to the cemetery but he got so scared that it caused his death. If I were that scared of something I'd probably find an excuse not to do it, but being made fun of would be very hard, too.*

**Evaluation:** This is a complete response to the question that asks what you would do in Ivan's place. The writer clearly explains the comparison between Ivan's situation and a similar situation that he or she faced and then goes on to explain how the outcome could have been different, but the writer changes his or her position from the first paragraph to the second. In the first, the writer says he or she would do the same things as Ivan. In the second paragraph, he or she says, "I'd find an excuse not to do it." The writer uses information from the story and draws conclusions based on personal experience.

**Question 12—Score 4 Response:** *If I had been in Ivan's place I would not have accepted the Lieutenant's challenge. I wouldn't want to be friends with people who made fun of me and didn't try to understand my fears. Ivan was too afraid of being an outsider. He should have been more independent. I would never accept such a silly bet or I would have accepted it under certain conditions.*

*I would have told the Lieutenant that I would go to the cemetery if he would go before me. That way I could see if it was safe. Or I would make sure that someone came looking for me if I didn't come right back. If Ivan had asked for someone to come find him if he didn't return in one hour, he would not have frozen to death. But he would have faced even more ridicule. Maybe Ivan would rather be dead than made fun of but I wouldn't want that. Once, I was with a group of friends who wanted to go ice-skating on a pond that we all knew we weren't allowed to be on. We snuck out with our skates. When we got to the lake I decided I didn't want to skate because I was afraid if my parents found out I'd get in trouble. My friends started calling me "sissy" but I didn't care. I knew if I fell in the lake and drowned it wouldn't matter what names they called me.*

**Evaluation:** This is a very complete response that extends the text into a real life situation. Information from the text is provided and the writer shows understanding of the feelings of the character, Ivan. The question is fully answered.

By now you can see the similarity between the high school format and the middle school format and the pattern to the question types. This can be an important piece of the puzzle when trying to help your child prepare for a state assessment test.

### STAND-ALONE WRITING

Just as the high school exams frequently require stand-alone writing, so do the middle school exams. These stand-alone prompts are frequently referred to as questions that generate text. That is, they require students to produce text rather than just read text or respond to it. Also, unlike text-based responding, stand-alone prompts have no multiple-choice questions. They do not lead students to identify main ideas or supporting details that can be transferred into a written response of their own. Stand-alone prompts truly require that students "stand alone" when they write.

In some states children are given visual prompts to stimulate their thinking. In New Jersey, for example, a photograph is used to inspire thinking. Visit the New Jersey State Education Department's website for an actual test question complete with photo and sample student responses (www.state.nj.us/njded/stass/index.html). Or, you can take a practice test by going to the LearningExpress website (www.LearnATest.com).

☛ **PARENT TIP:** Make it a habit to share newspapers and magazines with your child. Point out photos that look interesting and speculate about what could be happening or what did happen to the subjects in the photo. This is a good technique that fosters critical and creative thinking.

On some state middle school exams students are given two stand-alone prompts, one for narration and/or exposition and one for persuasion. Consider a recent Pennsylvania grade six writing assessment. The narrative prompt asked students to "Tell about a time when someone needed to be brave." The persuasive prompt asked youngsters to write to persuade a broadcaster not to cancel their favorite TV show. Both prompts gave students up to one hour to write and students were given very specific directions. A visit to the Pennsylvania State Education Department's website will give you sample student responses and scoring guidelines for both prompts (www.pde.psu.edu/pssa/esstand.html).

No matter how the standards are interpreted, the scoring guidelines are remarkably consistent. *Focus* (main idea, main point), *content* (details which support the main idea), *organization* (paragraphs which offer specific details which develop the main idea with logical transitions), *style* (word choice and sentence variety), and *conventions* (the mechanics of grammar and spelling) are the backbone of good writing.

☛ **PARENT TIP:** Ask your child's teacher for a copy of the writing rubric that is used to assess daily writing activities. Keep a copy posted on the refrigerator to remind you and your child of these important criteria.

Let's take a look at the following stand-alone prompt typical of a grade eight exam. It is a persuasive assignment.

Your friends and you have been discussing the amount of homework that you are assigned to complete each night. Some of your friends raised the concern that their backpacks have become health hazards because they are so heavy and they want to protest that they are required to carry too much weight back and forth to school every day. They have decided to write to the school board to protest the amount of homework and the weight of materials that they are given. You decide to write a letter as well.

Do you agree or disagree that you are assigned too much homework and that your book bag or backpack is too heavy? Prepare a letter for the next school board meeting in which you support a change in the homework policy of your school or support the policy as it exists. Be sure to give at least three good reasons to support your point.

**No Command—0 Points:** *What are back problems? What is life? Panes and soreness. My back is a rock. Homework crashes on my rock and fall away. Arching backwards, like a bridge of body, back, books. No life because back breaks beautifully. I wish I is free, vertical and lite.*

*Who are teachers to say I can not stand soft and straight. No back problems. No home. Life.*

**Evaluation:** Attempts to be creative while still meeting certain requirements are encouraged; however, when creativity interferes with certain objectives, then scores suffer. In this case, the reader can only speculate that the author is attempting a poetic response to the assignment. However, the response does not coherently address a question, nor does it address an audience. It might be poetic, but without any other support, the reader must assume the author does not have an adequate command of the written language to respond. Such a response could not be presented to a school board, nor could any audience understand the cryptic message except the author himself. Sentence fragments and spelling errors only make this response more difficult to understand.

**Limited Command—2 Points:** *This stupid. Why do teachers assign so much homework? They know kids need to get out and have fun. I mean you don't learn everything in school. There is a lot to learn outside of school to. And they tell us we need to get more involved in community service and volunteering stuff but they give us any time to do it. I don't need no history about some dead guy who put up that Wall in germany. Where is that going to get me. The wall is down—there is no more of that red scare stuff. We got be living off the street. I want to know how to make the dough—not how to sew or make rubber band cars or what phase the moon is waxing or waning to tomorrow. Show me the money; show me something I can use. No more homework! No more books!*

**Evaluation:** This response cannot be presented at a school board meeting: it does not address the issue of backpack related problems or the stress of homework. Consequently, it fails to comply with the assignment. The passage lacks a focus. Homework, though mentioned in the beginning, does not take precedence in the latter half of the response. Sentences are off-the-cuff, unsubstantiated, and unthoughtful. To disagree with school policy is acceptable as long as an intelligent argument is made. The lack of verbs and verb agreements interfere with readability. Mechanical and spelling mistakes also mar this argument. However, because it makes allusions to in school subjects and does express opinions, it scores more than a 0 or 1.

**Partial Command—3 Points:** *I really can't argue against all this homework and all these books I have to carry. Ocassionally my book bag gets realy awkward to carry, but I do not carry my bag all that often. I don't need to. I do most of my work in study hall and lunch. Sometimes*

*I take some reading home, but I rarely read that much. You don't have too—the teachers will read it to you in class anyway, or I just ask a friend what it was about. There are even Cliff notes. Its not really cheating—its just using your time better. I mean if people are getting really hurt then maybe they should take fewer classes or get an extra set of textbooks to leave at home. Or maybe they should get one of those pull-guys that look like suitcases I personally wouldn't be caught dead wheeling around my books, but if school means all that much to them, then they might as well. If I can get by without a big pack back, I can't see why they cannot. I also manage to work for my uncle 25 hours a week. So I think the school board should leave the homework and book thing alone.*

**Evaluation:** This response answers the task but is only moderately aware of the audience it is addressing; not until the very last sentence is there reference to the school board. There is a focus, but it is only very loosely developed. The writer does not feel that there is a need to carry backpacks to the point of back strain if one utilizes his or her time more effectively during school hours. Details in the passage are sporadically developed or inserted. However, he or she does provide two important alternatives to changing the homework policy.

Overall, the piece is short, paragraph development is weak, and supporting details are few.

**Adequate Command— 4 Points:** *Too many kids today do not appreciate the education that they get. It is very important to do all that you are asked to do in school so you can get a good job when you graduate. The school board has to be sure we get the best education and I want you to know that I think homework and book bags are not a big deal for us.*

*When my teachers give a big assignment they check with other teachers so that we don't have too many things due at the same time. Then the teachers make sure that our tests are on different days so we don't have to bring all our books home every day at the same time. This means that all those kids complaining about taking home all their books everyday are just not right. Some of my teachers, well really only one, lets us keep our books home all the time and we never use them in class.*

*I also think that homework is a good thing because some kids don't have a lot of activities after school and have nothing to do but watch TV. My mom says that if you watch a lot of TV it is very bad for you so I think homework is good. I wish I did better on my tests though because sometimes when I do homework I don't understand and there is no teacher there to help me.*

**Comments:** The piece starts off with a sense of the task and then wanders off. Though the writer provides two good explanations to support the appropriateness of homework and book distribution, neither point is fully developed. The piece further digresses when the writer talks about TV and needing teacher help.

The response is short and not adequately developed, but it has a good sense of audience and two good supporting details.

**Strong Command—5 Points:** *My backpack is absurdly heavy! By the time I graduate I'll have a hump as large as Victor Hugo's misunderstood monster of Notre Dame. As I pass crowds, people will point and snicker at the callus on my back that grew to look like its own continent. I have seven subjects a day; each subject demands a half-hour to an hour of homework a night— at the least that is three and a half hours of drudgery after a long day of school. Some of it is really absurd, too. For French, I have to write 40 words five times each and read the dreaded Hugo classic!*

*Not only have I developed a sore back I also have achy legs and knees, as well as a migraine problem. School is seriously bad for my physical well being! I remember when that white stuff that used to coat the pipes in the hallways was discovered to be cancer causing. School was shut down for a month while they removed it. When back problems and headaches become chronic enough, the school board must take immediate action.*

*Granted, you can not just scrape teachers off black boards as easily as you removed that carcinogen stuff, but putting a cap on some of the more exuberant and homework-heavy teachers would be appreciated. Then maybe I could have a life. I am on the lacrosse team, and I feel like the old man on the team because I am so tired during practice. Teachers do not realize that kids have other things that take up their time after school. I need time for practice and to have fun. Right now, all I do is work and carry that heavy book bag. My knees pop and I am only thirteen.*

**Evaluation:** This response answers the question and is very clear in its position. The introduction clearly states the problem. The conclusion could be stronger and relate back to the introductory paragraph.

This author uses exaggeration to express his disgust with book bags and homework. His language might border on the inappropriate for a school board member except that he appeals more to emotion than to logic which gives the piece its unique and creative edge. The writer could be more detailed about his experiences with backpacks, and he could offer even more examples of ineffective homework.

The writer also establishes the comparison between a former school health problem—asbestos—and the health concerns related to backpacks. Using precedents in this way is very effective, though there is a vast difference between carcinogens and popping knees.

The response is organized, focused, and on topic, though its use of supporting details could be stronger. The sense of audience could be stronger, and the appeal for action more clear.

**Superior Command—6 Points:** *I am an average student. I do most of my homework, and so I carry my share of textbooks between home and school. As "the average" I believe that I can speak honestly about the weight and impact of homework on both my spine and my social life.*

*On any given school day I guess I can carry 10–20 pounds of books to and from school. I am forced to carry all these books because I need them to do my homework and to study. I have never honestly weighed my backpack. I usually only weigh myself every morning and even then I take off my shoes to be even lighter. But I can tell you what I carry and you will see that it must weigh an awful lot! In addition to my books for homework I also carry my violin for orchestra. Obviously, I do not cram my instrument into my bag, but it is an additional burden I bear. I also carry five three-subject notebooks, complete with Xeroxes; a music folder; four text books, each about an inch wide or 300 pages (the paper backs do not weigh has much as the hard covers, but they flop a lot more in my bag); and the usual assortment of pens (3), pencils (2), and erasers; markers; a bottle of white out and makeup. Sometimes I bring another book or magazine to read during study hall. So the book bag I use can get hefty. Sometimes I feel like I am one of those souped up tractors at a truck pulled. On my back is that 10-ton sleigh not letting me go as far as I want. But that really isn't the case. Readjusting the bag on my shoulder or switching it side to side usually relieves some of the pressure. Double strapped backpacks with the buckle in front (the type designed for professional hikers) makes the books even less of a burden. Anyway, at the bus stop I set my bag on the ground, except on rainy days. Between classes I lighten the load by depositing some books in my locker. I feel it isn't necessary to carry all those books at once except on the way to and from school and even then I am not carrying them all because I am sitting on a bus or in a friend's car. So I really don't see why so many kids are complaining about their book burden.*

*As for homework—yes, it is the reason I carry so many books, but homework is unavoidable. Teachers have less than 40 minutes a day to teach us everything we need to know. Is that really enough time to not only explain an idea but also reinforce that idea? I do not think so, and neither does my sister who attends SUNY Geneseo. She constantly complains about being underprepared for college. The tedium of homework, as much as I hate to admit it, is a necessary evil. Vocabulary chapters may seem boring and repetitive; however, they are the most direct method of learning and relearning words until they stick in the head. As a student, I do not think I'd voluntarily review as much as homework makes me. I'd just go home and watch* Friends.

*As my parents are fond of telling me, I do not always know what is best for me. I trust teachers to give me the homework that they think will either challenge me or reinforce their lessons. Seeing as every subject and teacher is different, is it really practical to determine a single standard for everyone? Teachers are trained to make the decisions that meet the needs of their students (at least I hope they are). For once, I will agree to whatever they assign me and carry the necessary weight of their decisions.*

*So, I must agree with the homework policy and book requirements as they now are and I think the school board should leave it all alone.*

**Evaluation:** This response answers the question and fulfills the requirements of the task. There is a clear introduction and conclusion and the author responds to the task and fully answers the question. The piece displays command of the written language, a sense of humor and an eye for detail. The piece is well organized and focuses on the two points that need to be addressed: the weight of the backpack and the amount of homework. The language is appropriate in a letter to a school board member. The author's voice—shown in asides as she weighs herself—reveals a real person testifying to her real experiences. The argument for maintaining the homework policy is clearly expressed. The writer supports her argument using her sister's experiences as well as her own.

The response is well organized, focused, and uses good supporting details in a tone appropriate to the intended audience. The conventions of standard English are well controlled; there is good use of vocabulary and a variety of sentences.

Following are several other persuasive writing topics. Often, these topics will be the subject of a stand-alone writing prompt. Discuss these issues with your child to encourage the kind of thinking students need to do to tackle this kind of writing task.

- ► Dress codes
- ► Cell phone and beeper use
- ► Curfew times
- ► School prayer
- ► Locker searches
- ► Zero tolerance policies
- ► Attendance policies

Now let's take a look at the mathematics assessment that your child will take in middle school.

# Looking at Middle School Exams: Mathematics

**Just as** there is remarkable similarity in the English/Language Arts Assessment Tests, so is there similarity in the mathematics tests. Each state's content standards are designed to move students through a carefully developed program of study that builds on the skills acquired from one year to the next. In other words, the category of Number Sense and Concepts may expect K-2 students to use place value concepts to represent whole numbers using numerals, words, and physical models. But by the end of third and fourth grade, students will be expected to use the place value structure of the base-ten number system to read, write, represent, and compare whole numbers and decimals. In grades five through seven, students are expected to understand number concepts including place value, exponents, prime and composite numbers, multiples, and factors; fractions, decimals, percents, integers, and numbers in scientific notation by translating among equivalent forms; and compare and order numbers within a set.

By the end of the twelfth grade, number sense has been advanced into discrete mathematics, trigonometry, and other more sophisticated math concepts and applications.

However, the four basic categories remain the same throughout the grades. (See Chapter 4, pages 74–75.) They are:

1. Number Sense and Concepts
2. Spatial Sense and Geometry
3. Data Analysis, Probability and Statistics, and Discrete Mathematics
4. Patterns, Functions, and Algebra

The only thing that changes is the age and grade appropriate expectations within the categories. And after it has all been broken down into grade level expectations, it has to be translated into actual classroom experience. So let's take a look at what a middle school teacher might ask students to do in the category of probability and statistics.

The Minnesota Department of Children, Families & Learning website (www.educ. state.mn.us) lists the following as student expectations in middle school for Chance and Data Handling (Category 3):

A student shall:

1. evaluate and solve problems—including calculating basic measures of center and variability—to demonstrate understanding of basic concepts of probability and calculate simple probabilities.
2. formulate a question and design an appropriate data investigation.
3. organize raw data and represent it in more than one way.
4. analyze data by selecting and applying appropriate data measurement concepts.
5. critique various representations of data.
6. devise and conduct a simulated probability situation.
7. predict future results based on experimental results.

The Minnesota website then offers an example of a classroom project to teach to Category 3, and it gives its expectation for student performance:

**Classroom Task**
1. Play a dice game with a partner.
   The rules of the game: The game is played by two students, each of whom has one six-sided die. The students roll the dice simultaneously and find the absolute or positive value of the difference of the numbers. Student A wins if the value is 0, 1, or 2; student B wins if the value is 3, 4, or 5. For example, if A

rolls a 4 and B rolls a 5, the difference is 1 and A wins. However, if A rolls a 2 and B rolls a 6, the difference is 4 and B wins.

2. Review and study the rules. Imagine that players had all afternoon to play the game. In your notebook, *predict* whether the game would favor player A or player B or is fair to both players. Use theoretical probability to help explain how to predict future results.

3. Test your prediction. As a class, play the game in pairs ten times. Write every pair's results on the board.

4. Examine the results (data) on the board. In your notebook, *explain* what the results (data) suggest. Predict what results one would get if the game continued. Give suggestions of how the game could change to make it fair.

5. Construct a "fair" game involving two dice or a variation of the game just played. Write the rules in your notebook.

6. Play the new game and verify if it is, indeed, fair. Show the results of your play in a tally or table. Explain in a paragraph how experimental results were used to predict future results.

In Category 2, Spatial Sense and Geometry, called "Space, Shape, and Measurement" in Minnesota, the following are suggested classroom activities for students:

1. Students complete several drawings that lead to parts of a backyard design, including flower beds, sprinkler set-up, and storage shed. They will also explore seven dimension changes of a shipping box and angles of a clock face.

2. Students create a simple patio design and a more complex design to demonstrate their knowledge of tessellation. They also draw a coordinate graph to show transformations.

3. Students design and construct models of two storage sheds; one with a sloped roof and the other with a flat roof. They test how much weight each roof will hold.

These activities are "real-world" examples, so how does all this become state test questions at the middle school level? It's easy to understand. Following are the four categories broken down into sample test questions. As was the case with high school math and ELA, middle school standards are as variable as the 50 states. However, most states test math with grid-in (multiple-choice) and extended (show your work) problems.

Topics include:

- ▶ Operations with rational numbers
- ▶ Percents
- ▶ Proportions and ratios
- ▶ Scientific notation and standard form
- ▶ Powers and roots

1. What is the standard form of $6.2 \times 10^4$?
   a. .00062
   b. .620
   c. 6,200
   d. 62,000

The correct answer is **d.** To convert scientific notation to standard form, multiply 6.2 by $10^4$. Since $10^4$ = 10,000, you just multiply 6.2 by 10,000 = 6.2 × 10,000 = 6,200. When converting scientific notation to standard form, remember that positive numbers of ten require you to move the decimal to the right the same number of spaces as the power of ten. Negative powers of ten require you to move the decimal to the left.

This question requires the student to convert from scientific notation to standard form. Eighth graders are expected to convert scientific notation to standard form and standard form to scientific notation.

2. What fraction of the figure below is shaded?

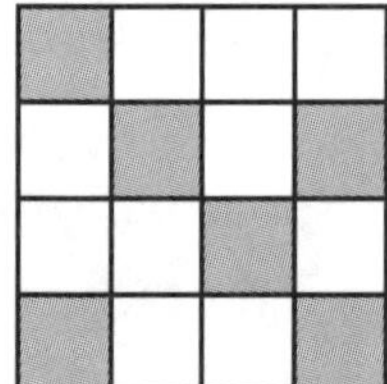

   a. $\frac{5}{16}$
   b. $\frac{3}{4}$
   c. $\frac{1}{2}$
   d. $\frac{3}{8}$

The correct answer is **d.** 6 of 16 squares are shaded. $\frac{6}{16} = \frac{3}{8}$.

This question tests recognizing fractions and reducing fractions to simplest form, a basic concept for eighth graders.

3. Paul works for a toy manufacturer. If 10 crates can hold 480 boxed dolls, which proportion can be used to determine the number of boxed dolls, *d*, that 6,200 crates can hold?

a. $\frac{10}{d} = \frac{6{,}200}{480}$

b. $\frac{10}{480} = \frac{d}{6{,}200}$

c. $\frac{d}{6{,}200} = \frac{480}{10}$

d. $\frac{6{,}200}{d} = \frac{480}{10}$

The correct answer is **c**. The ratio of *d* to 6,200 will equal the ratio of 10 to 480. Set these two ratios equal to each other in order to make a proportion:

$$\frac{d}{6{,}200} = \frac{10}{480}$$

This is equivalent to choice **c**.

This question tests the student's ability to set up a proportion. Other proportion questions may also require the eighth grader to solve for a numerical answer.

4. What is 75% of 80?

a. 60

b. 75

c. 40

d. 20

The correct answer is **a**. 75% of 80 is just $\frac{3}{4}$ of 80. $\frac{3}{4} \times 80 = 60$.

This question tests application of percents. On the eighth grade level, students should be able to quickly access the fractional equivalent of percents. In this example, taking three-fourths of 80 leads to a quick solution.

### SPATIAL SENSE AND GEOMETRY

Topics include:

▶ Calculating perimeters, areas, and volumes of common plane figures and 3-D solids

▶ Pythagorean Theorem

▶ Similar figures

▶ Right triangle trigonometry

▶ Estimation strategies

▶ Transformations

▶ Coordinate geometry

**1.** Which answer choice describes how to transform ΔABC into ΔDEF?

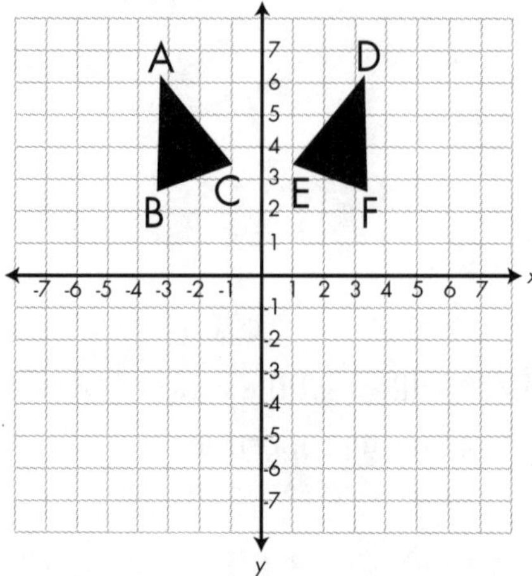

    **a.** ΔABC was rotated about the *y*-axis

    **b.** ΔABC was dilated

    **c.** ΔABC was reflected about the *x*-axis

    **d.** ΔABC was reflected about the *y*-axis

The correct answer is **d.** A reflection or mirror image is a flip. Here ΔABC was flipped over the vertical, or *y*, axis. A rotation is a turn and dilation is a proportional change in size.

This question tests the knowledge of transformations and the orientation of the coordinate *x* and *y* axes. Eighth graders should know the following transformations:

- reflection
- rotation
- dilation
- translation

 A PARENT'S GUIDE TO HIGH STAKES TESTING

2. If ΔABC and ΔDEF are similar and the perimeter if ΔABC = 16, what is the perimeter of ΔDEF?

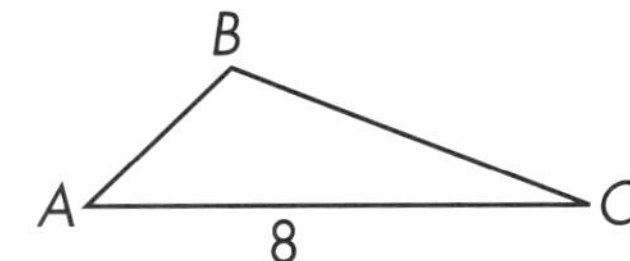


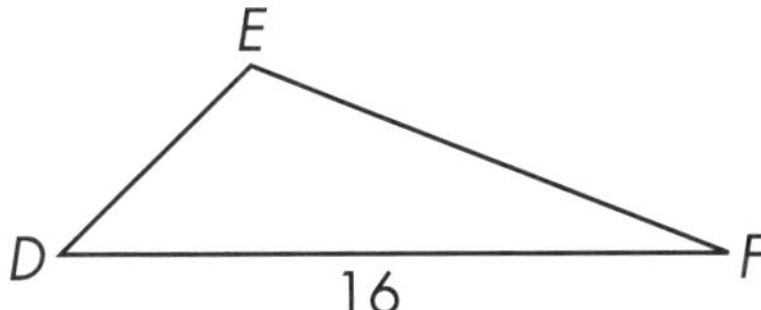


a. 24

b. 32

c. 48

d. It cannot be determined by the information given.

The correct answer is **b.** AC = 8 and DF = 16, so the larger triangle has sides that are double the lengths of the sides of the smaller triangle. The perimeter of this larger triangle will also be double the smaller triangles perimeter. $2 \times 16 = 32$. This is a fundamental geometry question for eighth graders.

3. What are the coordinates of point D?

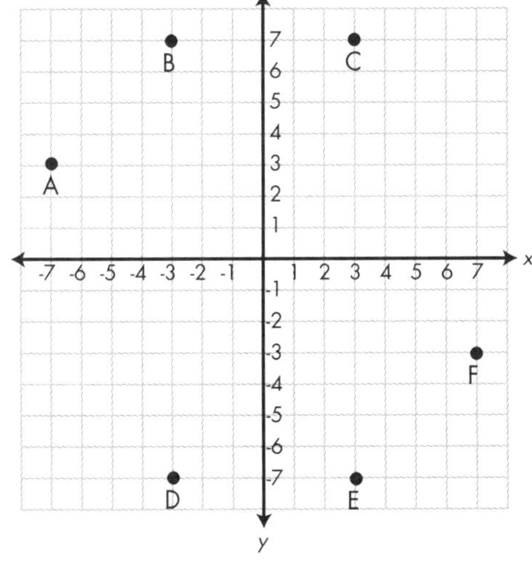


a. (3,7)

b. (−3,−7)

c. (3,−7)

d. (−3,7)

The correct answer is **b.** Coordinates are listed in the form $(x,y)$ where $x$ is the horizontal distance and $y$ is the vertical distance. Point D has an $x$ coordinate of –3 and a $y$ coordinate of –7. Thus, choice **b** (–3,–7) is the correct answer.

This question tests the student's knowledge of the coordinate plane and how to plot points on that plane. At the eighth grade level, students are expected to plot and read points off the grid. They are expected to be able to draw a line when given a table of coordinates and to figure out the equation of that line by examining the drawing they made. This sets the stage for students to use $y = mx + b$ to plot lines when they get to high school.

4. If angle C below equals 90, which of the following statements is true?

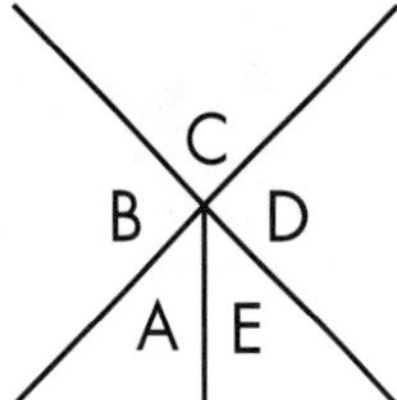

   **a.** Angles A and E are supplementary.
   **b.** Angles C and D are complementary.
   **c.** Angles A and E are complementary.
   **d.** Angles B and A are supplementary.

The correct answer is **c.** Complementary angles add to 90 degrees. A and E form a right angle (90°) and are thus complementary. Supplementary angles add to 180°.

This question requires the test taker to spot right angles and to be familiar with the following terminology, all part of the foundation for high school mathematics:

▶ supplementary
▶ complementary

Topics include:

- ▶ Theoretical and experimental probability
- ▶ Compound events (dependent and independent)
- ▶ Mean, median, and mode
- ▶ Graphing data (circle graphs, bar graphs, histograms, tables, stem-and-leaf plots)
- ▶ Simple combinations
- ▶ Simple permutations

1. (Short Answer) The Washington School Student Council will choose one student at random to accept an award on behalf of their school. If the student council consists of 8 freshmen, 12 sophomores, 13 juniors, and 15 seniors:

   **Part A:** What is the probability that a freshman will be chosen?

   **Part B:** What is the probability that a senior will NOT be chosen?

Answer:

**Part A:** There are a total of 48 students (8 + 12 + 13 + 15 = 48). 8 are freshmen. So the probability that a freshman will get picked is 8 out of 48. $\frac{8}{48} = \frac{1}{6}$.
(Note: $\frac{8}{48}, \frac{4}{24}, \frac{2}{12}, \frac{1}{6}$ are all acceptable answers.)

**Part B:** 15 are seniors, so the students who are not seniors would be 48 − 15 = 33. The probability that a senior would not be chosen is $\frac{33}{48}$.

2. Mary, Jane, Natasha, and Todd will stand in a line. How many different arrangements are possible?
   a. 12
   b. 16
   c. 24
   d. 32

The correct answer is **c.** To find the total number of arrangements of 4 "elements," use $4! = 4 \times 3 \times 2 \times 1 = 24$.

**3.** Mrs. Jackson's eighth grade class took a survey in order to determine what kind of snack they should choose for their party. 25% chose cupcakes, 15% chose pizza, 20% chose cookies, and 40% chose ice cream. Which pie chart below best represents the data that Mrs. Jackson's class collected?

**a.**

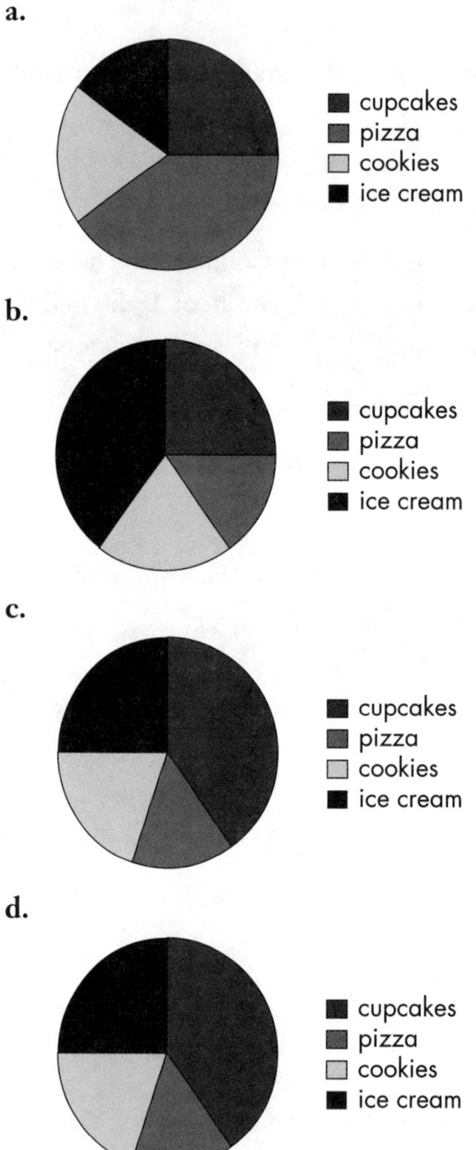


**b.**



**c.**



**d.**



The correct answer is **b.** 40% chose ice cream, so the largest section of the pie should be black. This segment will also be slightly less than $\frac{1}{2}$ (50 percent) of the circle. The next largest slice should be $\frac{1}{4}$ of the pie. This represents the 25% ($\frac{1}{4}$) that chose cupcakes. Cookies would be a smaller slice (20%) and pizza (15%) should be the smallest slice. Only choice **b** shows this scenario.

This question requires an eighth grader to choose which pie chart shows the data being presented. It combines number concepts (percents and relating percents to fractions) with data analysis and representation.

4. Mr. Avery made a table to show the number of days each student was absent from his class. What was the median number of days absent for the students shown?

| Student Name | Days Absent |
| --- | --- |
| Abigail | 7 |
| Matt | 5 |
| Jade | 4 |
| Jaclyn | 6 |
| Theresa | 8 |
| Damian | 3 |
| John | 4 |
| Anthony | 4 |
| Mark | 9 |

   a. 4
   b. 5
   c. 6
   d. 7

The correct answer is **b.** To find the median, first arrange the numbers in order: 3 4 4 4 5 6 7 8 9

The middle value is the median. Here, the median is 5: 3 4 4 4 *5* 6 7 8 9

Note that the mode is 4. The mode is the number that occurs the most frequently.

This question requires the student to read a table (data analysis) and to use the information presented in order to determine the median. An eighth grader is expected to be able to determine the following values when analyzing data:

▶ mean (average)
▶ median
▶ mode
▶ range
▶ minimum
▶ maximum

Topics include:

▶ Number patterns

▶ Linear functions

▶ Creating and manipulating algebraic equations

**1.** (Short Answer) Given $\frac{b}{15} + 2 = -3$, solve for $b$.

Answer:

$$\frac{b}{15} + 2 = -3$$
$$\underline{\quad -2 \quad\quad -2} \text{ (Subtract 2 from both sides)}$$
$$\frac{b}{15} \quad\quad = -5$$

$$\frac{b}{15} \times 15 = -5 \times 15 \text{ (Multiply both sides by 15)}$$
$$b \quad\quad\quad = -75$$

This algebra question focuses on isolating a variable and manipulating an equation. Remember, when solving for or isolating a variable, you must make your calculations exactly the same on both sides of the equation.

**2.** Which inequality is represented by the number line below?

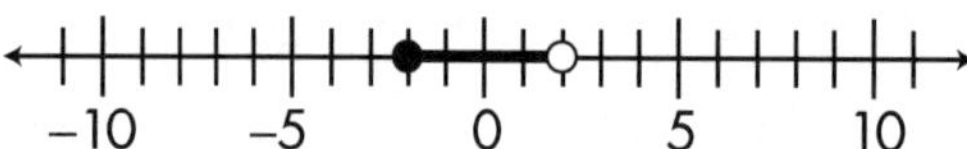


**a.** $-2 < x < 2$

**b.** $-2 \leq x \leq 2$

**c.** $-2 \leq x < 2$

**d.** $-2 < x \leq 2$

The correct answer is **c.** Because the circle at the point $-2$ is black, $x$ can equal $-2$. $x$ can also be any value greater than $-2$ and less than 2. The open circle at the point 2 tells us that $x$ cannot be 2. Thus, the inequality would be $-2 \leq x < 2$.

3. What will the value of *y* be when *x* = 7? *Refer to the function table below.*

| x | y |
|---|---|
| 0 | 2 |
| 1 | 5 |
| 2 | 8 |
| 3 | 11 |
| 4 | 14 |

a. 23

b. 17

c. 9

d. 4

The correct answer is **a.** The equation for *y* is $y = 3x + 2$. You can determine this equation by examining the values in both columns and seeing if the equation you come up with applies to all of the values shown. Thus, when $x = 7$, *y* would equal $(3)(7) + 2 = 21 + 2 = 23$.

This question is a more advanced version of the In-Out tables students see in elementary school. Function tables show the *x* and *y* values for a formula $y = f(x)$. In other words the *y* values (dependent variables) are a function of the *x* variables (independent variables). Eighth grade students should be familiar with:

▶ functions

▶ independent variables

▶ dependent variables

▶ domain

▶ range

4. Which choice below contains a number that will make the equation $3y + 5 = 2y$ hold true?

a. 5

b. 4

c. −5

d. −4

The correct answer is **c.** To solve, isolate the variable:

$$3y + 5 = 2y$$
$$\underline{-3y \qquad -3y} \text{ (subtract } 3y \text{ from both sides)}$$
$$5 = -y$$
$$-1 \times 5 = -y \times -1 \text{ (multiply both sides by } -1)$$
$$-5 = y$$

Thus, choice **c** is the answer. Alternatively, this question may be solved by putting the answer choices into the given equation in order to see which one holds true. Here, (3)(–5) + 5 = 2(5) becomes –15 + 5 = 10, and finally 10 = 10, which is true.

This algebra question deals with substitution and also solving equations.

## Annual Testing and Scientifically Based Research

THE GOAL FOR all 50 states by the end of the 2005–2006 school year, as required by the new *No Child Left Behind Act*, is to administer English/Language Arts standards-based assessments annually in grades three through eight. *Education Week*, the national newspaper dealing with educational issues, recently published an article by Lynn Olson, entitled "Testing Systems in Most States Not ESEA Ready" (January 9, 2002 issue). According to the article, there are only nine states that are in compliance with the testing requirement (California, Delaware, Florida, Georgia, Mississippi, North Carolina, South Carolina, Texas, and Utah). Thirty-seven other states are well on their way by offering standards-based tests in English/Language Arts and math at least once in elementary school (grades 3–5), middle school (grades 6–8), and high school (grades 9–12). The remaining four (District of Columbia, Tennessee, West Virginia, and Wisconsin) use norm-referenced tests but are working to move to standards-based instruments.

The rationale for this annual testing in grades three through eight is to provide data to measure student performance, school performance, and district performance and then implement policies and procedures to correct weaknesses and build on strengths. However, before huge sums of money are spent on programs or textbooks or curriculum writing or teacher training, the *No Child Left Behind Act* mandates that *scientifically based research* must be used to evaluate the effectiveness of "what works." Following is the definition of scientifically based research as it appears in the *No Child Left Behind Act:*

"The term scientifically based research (A) means research that involves the application of rigorous, systematic, and objective procedures to obtain reliable and valid knowledge relevant to education activities and programs; and (B) includes research that:

- employs systematic, empirical methods that draw on observation or experiment
- involves rigorous data analyses that are adequate to test the stated hypotheses and justify the general conclusions drawn
- relies on measurements or observational methods that provide reliable and valid data across evaluators and observers, across multiple meas-

urements and observations, and across studies by the same or different investigators

- is evaluated using experimental or quasi-experimental designs in which individuals, entities, programs, or activities are assigned to different conditions and with appropriate controls to evaluate the effects of the condition of interest, with a preference for random-assignment experiments, or other designs to the extent that those designs contain within-condition or across-condition controls
- ensures that experimental studies are presented in sufficient detail and clarity to allow for replication or, at a minimum, offer the opportunity to build systematically on their findings
- has been accepted by a peer-reviewed journal or approved by a panel of independent experts through a comparably rigorous, objective, and scientific review"

This definition applies primarily to the research that will be conducted to "prove" that school improvement programs or other initiatives will work to improve below standard or failing schools. No school district can afford to spend thousands of dollars or sacrifice thousands of children to programs with no proven success rate. That's where the scientifically-based part comes in. With such a safeguard in place, there is some measure of security for educators hoping to reform underachieving schools.

This takes us right back to high stakes testing. Ultimately, the results of the standards-based testing—which the *No Child Left Behind Act* requires—will drive school reform; therefore these standards-based tests themselves must be scientifically based. The premise on which standards-based testing relies is that, if the standards are clearly stated and curriculum is aligned to teaching practices, then tests can measure the accomplishment of the standards. At that point, the test results should be accurate indicators of student performance.

Now let's look at where it all begins. Elementary language arts and math follow in the next two chapters.

# Looking at Elementary School Exams: English/ Language Arts

**A clearly** articulated K-12 curriculum in English/Language Arts will define grade level expectations and performance indicators that will build one upon the other from grade to grade. So just as there is similarity between the test instruments in grades eight and ten/eleven, there will be consistency in the test format for the grade three/four test(s). In other words, the elementary program of instruction will begin building to the high school exit requirements. That means that reading, writing, listening, and speaking will be emphasized and that the grade three/four test(s) will be similar in format to both the middle school and the high school tests.

Did you notice how we are now talking about grades three and four? In elementary school, reading and writing are often separated. The reading comprehension test will be given in grade three, and the writing test in grade four. That doesn't mean that there may not be a writing section, as in open-ended questions, on the grade three reading test. But the stand-alone essays may be given a year later in grade four or even grade five.

For example, in New Jersey, the Elementary School Performance Assessment (ESPA) has reading comprehension that is text based, uses both fiction and nonfiction, and requires students to respond to both multiple-choice and open-ended written responses to questions. In addition, students have to answer two stand-alone writing activities. Students take this test in grade four.

Similarly, in Ohio, both the reading comprehension test and writing test are given in grade four. In North Carolina, however, students are tested in grade three for reading and then in grade five for writing. In Florida students are tested in reading and writing in grade four. In Delaware students are tested in both reading and writing in grades three and five. And the list could go on for all fifty states.

However, common to all English/Language Arts testing at any grade are the basic categories, sometimes called domains or content clusters, that require students to read, write, listen, and speak. These domains are:

- ► to identify the main idea
- ► to summarize
- ► to use a graph or chart to locate data
- ► to retell (paraphrase) a story in his or her own words
- ► to define vocabulary in context
- ► to draw inferences
- ► to recognize literary conventions
- ► to predict outcomes
- ► to recognize cause/effect and comparison/contrast (organization patterns)
- ► to apply information to personal writing

What distinguishes the elementary from the middle or high school assessments is that the passages will be less complex, shorter, and the writing will not include *persuasion* as a purpose.

For example, for full length, stand-alone writing, elementary students will write for 25 instead of 45 or 50 minutes, and they will be expected to satisfy less stringent rubrics. They will also be expected to write for narration or exposition (explanation) but *not* for persuasion.

In reading comprehension, informational pieces are used for the open-ended writing test. Students have to apply the information that they have learned from the passage as they write to respond. For reading comprehension that uses literary pieces, students will demonstrate that they can read beyond the text and interpret what they have read.

So, just as you saw in the middle and high school categories, in elementary English/Language Arts the categories are the same. It's just the test complexity that changes. Let's look at a nonfiction passage that might be used on a fourth grade reading test. Students are asked to read for information and understanding and then apply the facts and details of what they have read to both multiple-choice and open-ended questions.

## *Belle's On Call*

*By Amy McRary*
*Knoxville News Sentinel Reporter*

A dog named Belle has been called a "hero" by the Tennessee Animal Hall of Fame. She is four years old. She is a yellow Labrador retriever. She is a professionally trained service dog, and she has been the companion of Angela Pettry for two years. Angela is unable to walk because she was hurt in an automobile accident. Belle has been her biggest helper.

Belle knows almost 100 commands. She can "come" or "stay" but she can also turn on a light switch or open the refrigerator door. The refrigerator handle has a rope tied to it. Belle can pull on the rope to open the door. She does the same thing with Angela's other doors. Belle can even open the drawers on Angela's desk.

If Angela drops a pencil, Belle picks it up and drops it into her owner's hand. Belle even helps Angela take off her coat. The dog uses her mouth to pull Angela's coat off her arms. "It's like tug of war to her," says Angela. One of Belle's favorite jobs is opening the mailbox and getting the mail for Angela.

Angela and Belle became partners in 1996. Angela found out about The Canine Assistance Program, which trains dogs to help disabled people. The Canine Assistance Program does not charge money for the dogs but it costs over $10,000 to train the dogs.

Belle's life was not always a happy one. When she was four months old she was left at an animal shelter. The animal shelter gave her to the Canine Assistance program because Labrador retrievers are very smart and easy to train. They are very friendly with people. But after her training Belle could not get an owner. One owner was selected but then brought Belle back because he didn't like her. Then another person brought Belle back. Then Angela came, and it was love at first sight.

The love between Angela and Belle came right away. It was as if the dog knew this was her chance. Today, Belle is very much loved and very much needed. Belle travels with Angela everywhere. When they go an airplane Belle sits in the seat right next to Angela. When Angela goes to work Belle has a special bed right under Angela's desk. In case Angela needs her, Belle is always right there. Assistance dogs are not considered "pets." They are considered "workers" so they are allowed to go places where ordinary animals are not allowed to go, even the supermarket. Belle even goes food shopping with Angela.

The job that Belle does best is to help Angela make friends. "People are afraid of someone who has a handicap. When you are in a wheelchair, people aren't always very nice to you," says Angela. But Belle changed all that. People love to reach out and pet her beautiful gold fur. Children love to talk to Belle, and if you talk to Belle you have to talk to Angela. Belle is always the center of attention wherever Angela goes and because of Belle, Angela is no longer lonely.

Belle's favorite place to be is right on Angela's lap. The big dog stretches the front half of her body across Angela and sleeps peacefully. Angela calls Belle a "person with fur" because she loves and respects her best friend. Angela and Belle are buddies.

*Adapted from the* Knoxville News Sentinel *with permission.*

MULTIPLE-CHOICE QUESTIONS

1. Belle is
    a. a disabled person.
    b. a Labrador retriever.
    c. a girlfriend.
    d. a doctor.

The correct answer is **b.** This is a literal question, and the answer can be found directly in the text.

2. Angela found Belle
   a. on the street.
   b. at the animal shelter.
   c. at the Canine Assistance Program.
   d. at the pet store.

The correct answer is **c.** This is a literal question and the answer can be found directly in the text.

3. What is one of Belle's favorite things to do?
   a. go for a walk in the park
   b. help Angela take off her coat
   c. eat her favorite dog food
   d. play with other dogs

The correct answer is **b.** This is a literal question and the answer can be found directly in the text.

4. Why does Angela call Belle "a person with fur?"
   a. Angela loves and respects Belle just like she would a person.
   b. Belle is really a human being dressed like a dog.
   c. Belle does tricks that are hard for a dog to do.
   d. Belle likes to be friends with people.

The correct answer is **a.** Even though the last paragraph states something similar, choice **a** paraphrases the response.

5. Why is Belle allowed to go everywhere with Angela?
   a. Angela refuses to go without her.
   b. Belle requires too much attention.
   c. Angela always gets special permission to take Belle with her.
   d. Belle is considered a working dog, and the rules about "no pets allowed" do not apply to her.

The correct answer is **d.** This question requires students to look at supporting details and then paraphrase the information provided in paragraph six.

On the elementary reading comprehension tests, many of the multiple-choice questions will be literal. With questions like these, children are being taught to identify key pieces of information as they read. They will then have the opportunity to apply that information to an open-ended prompt like this:

**6.** Assistance dogs can be very important helpers for disabled people. Explain how assistance dogs help their owners.

**OPEN-ENDED QUESTION SAMPLE RESPONSES**

The following sample answers would be scored using a rubric (set of criteria) specific for grade four students. The criteria would be very similar to the important qualities of writing that appear on a high school rubric:

- ▶ Organization
- ▶ Focus
- ▶ Style
- ▶ Conventions of standard English

But for a fourth grader, "organization" or "focus" would be measured much more simply than for a high school paper. Fourth graders are not expected to have a sophisticated writing style. For example, basic to all text-based writing would be whether or not the student demonstrates an understanding of the text. Organization for a fourth grader would be directed to the student's ability to stay on topic and to use supporting details. Focus would consider whether or not the student used facts from the text with accuracy.

Let's look at the following responses to the open-ended question above about Belle. Using a four-point scale with four being the highest score, answers would look like this:

**Question 6—Score 0 Response:** *My dog is my friend he love to play with me in the park and we found him at the pound.*

**Evaluation:** To score a 0, a paper is often blank or illegible or totally off topic.

**Question 6—Score 1 Response:** *Dogs are fun pets but some dogs do funny things like play all day and their owners need them to help them. Big dogs and expecially labrador dogs are good helpers because they can pick up things that you drop and they can open things if you can't. Dogs cost lots of money and they go places with you.*

**Evaluation:** This piece tries to answer the question ("owners need them to help") but is clearly way off the topic. Few details from the text are used and the facts are not accurate (dogs cost lots of money). There is little organization and the focus is missing. The writer has just taken bits and pieces (fragments) from the text and there is no unifying idea.

**Question 6—Score 2 Response:** *A dog that got left in a shelter couldn't find a home till a lady in a wheelchair came and got her. Then they became friends and the lady let the dog do tricks like pick up things and take off her coat and open the refrigerator and this dog goes all the places the lady goes like on airplanes and to the store. The dog cost the lady $10,000 because it was so smart. The lady really loves her dog because it is such a smart dog and she likes to show her off to children and people.*

**Evaluation:** This response attempts to answer the question but it does not demonstrate full understanding of the text. The writer focuses on what the dog can do, but not on the helping nature of the "tricks." Details are also misapplied and misstated such as "the dog cost the lady $10,000," and "the lady loves the dog because it is smart." The writer addresses some of the task but does not fully answer the question.

**Question 6—Score 3 Response:** *Dogs that are trained to help people are very smart and very helpful. These dogs can do lots of things like open doors and pick up things that get dropped. They help people do things that they can't do without them.*

*Dogs that work are called assistant dogs because they are allowed to go everywhere to help. They ride on airplanes and go to stores. They even go to work with their people.*

*Work dogs make friends and give a lot of love. They are very helpful.*

**Evaluation:** This piece also demonstrates understanding of the text, and there are no major errors in the facts that are used. Unlike the 4-point response, the 3-point response has fewer details, and it does not go beyond the text to add personal experience.

**Question 6—Score 4 Response:** *Assistance dogs are animals that help their owners do things that they can't do for themselves. If a person can't walk, an assistance dog can help pull the wheelchair. If the dog is like Belle, then that dog can be trained to do lots of things like fetch and open doors.*

*Most of these dogs are Labrador retrievers because they are the smartest and easiest to train. But one of the most important ways that dogs help disabled people is to make friends for them. People come up to them and talk to them about their dogs and then the disabled person doesn't feel so lonely.*

*Assistance dogs are allowed to go everywhere with their owners so they can help all the time. I once met a dog with a blind man and the dog was very nice to his friend and to me. Assistance dogs are friends for disabled people.*

**Evaluation:** This piece demonstrates understanding of the text, and there are no errors in the information the student has selected to use. The writing responds to the question and has a beginning and a conclusion related to the question. The 4-point response also goes outside the text to add personal experience.

Here are three additional possible open-ended questions for "Belle's On Call" which might be used on a fourth grade exam. See how your child does.

- ▶ Explain what Angela means when she says that Belle is "a person with fur."
- ▶ Explain how Belle helps Angela overcome her handicap.
- ▶ Tell about a time when you really needed a good friend.

Now let's look at a reading comprehension passage that uses literary text and is appropriate for third grade.

## *The Dog and the Wolf*
*An Aesop fable retold by Edith Wagner*

A very thin, very hungry wolf happened to meet a very fat, very well fed dog. After they greeted one another, the wolf asked the dog, "How can you look so good? Your fur is shiny and soft. Your food must be very healthy and tasty. I have to struggle to find enough food to eat. My fur is dull and dirty."

The dog looked at the wolf and felt very sorry for him. So he decided to tell him how to be well fed and happy. The dog said, "If you want to eat lots of food and live as well as I do, then you have to act the way I do."

The wolf was very interested. He knew he could do anything he needed to do if it meant that he would have plenty of good food to eat.

"What do I have to do?" asked the wolf.

"All you have to do is watch over the master's house every night and protect it from burglars," said the dog.

The wolf thought that this would be a very easy way to have enough food to eat and a warm place to sleep. He couldn't wait for his fur to look shiny and clean. So he told the dog that he would gladly join him and go to the master's house to stand guard. The wolf told the dog that living in the forest was a terrible thing for him. When it rained he got wet and cold and he always felt hungry. He was looking forward to his new life.

As they began jogging back to the master's house, the wolf noticed a mark on the dog's neck. He asked the dog what the mark was.

"Oh, it's nothing," said the dog.

"Then tell me about it," said the wolf.

The dog told the wolf that the mark on his neck came from the collar that he wore during the day. He explained that he needed the collar so his master could fasten a chain to it.

"A chain!" asked the wolf in alarm. "Why do you wear a chain?"

"I'm a guard dog. Sometimes people are afraid of me, so my master must keep me chained. But it's nothing to me. I'm always free to roam at night, and my master treats me very well. He feeds me from his plate and I am treated well by everyone in the house. But, wait. Where are you going?"

The wolf had turned around and was going off in a different direction.

"So long, friend. You may have shiny fur and a full belly but I'd rather be hungry and free than well fed and *chained*!"

**MULTIPLE-CHOICE QUESTIONS**

1. Why did the dog feel sorry for the wolf?
    a. The wolf was injured.
    b. The wolf looked very sick and old.
    c. The wolf was very thin and very hungry.
    d. The wolf scared the dog.

The correct answer is **c**. Though it is not stated directly in the text, it is implied that the dog felt sorry for the wolf because he recognized that the wolf was unhappy and hungry.

2. Why did the wolf turn around and leave the dog?
    a. He didn't want to leave his old home.
    b. He realized that he would be giving up his freedom.
    c. He was afraid of new places.
    d. He was afraid of being beaten.

The correct answer is **b**. This is not stated directly in the text, but it is implied that though the wolf was starving he knew he could not wear a chain around his neck, even for just a few hours every day.

3. What is the main purpose of this story?
    a. to tell a story about being hungry
    b. to make people laugh
    c. to teach a lesson about being free
    d. to teach about living in the forest

The correct answer is **c.** This is a fable and the story has a lesson to teach. The lesson is that being well fed and cared for requires that you have to pay for those luxuries. The wolf did not want to sacrifice his freedom for food and shelter; he thought the price was too high.

4. Why was the dog surprised that the wolf turned around?
    a. The dog did not understand freedom could be better than food and shelter.
    b. The dog thought that the weather was too cold for the wolf .
    c. The dog expected the wolf to be just like him.
    d. The dog didn't know that the wolf had found a better place to live.

The correct answer is **a.** Although it is not stated in the text, the dog clearly thinks that giving up his freedom in the daytime is a small price to pay for food and shelter. He cannot understand why the wolf would not want to live just as he does.

5. What is the best meaning of *chained* in the wolf's statement:
    ***"I'd rather be hungry and free than well fed and* chained."**
    a. restricted
    b. abused
    c. loved
    d. hated

The correct answer is **a.**

Questions about literature ask students to probe more deeply beyond the literal information supplied in the text. Questions about motive and message dominate. Here is what an open-ended question and four responses for a literature selection might look like:

6.   The dog and the wolf have made choices. Explain the choices they have made.

## OPEN-ENDED QUESTION SAMPLE RESPONSES

**Question 6—Score 0 Response:** *My dog looks like a wolf but he is nice and we play all the time like when we go in the back and I feed him and he runs after the ball.*

**Evaluation:** A zero paper is blank, illegible or totally off the task.

**Question 6—Score 1 Response:** *The dog and the wolf are friends and they choose to be friends even though they don't always like to be. The wolf wants to go to the dog's house and eat dinner but the dog wants to play in the woods and then go home when it gets dark. The wolf wants to be pretty but he is ugly. The dog wants to eat but the wolf has no food for him.*

**Evaluation:** The writer tries to answer the question and even shows some understanding of the story but the ideas are confused, and the references to the story are totally inaccurate.

**Question 6—Score 2 Response:** *The wolf and the dog are friends and the dog wants the wolf to come live with him. The wolf thinks it's a good idea but then he changes his mind and he chooses to go back to the forest.*

*The dog really wanted his friend to see his house and let his master feed him but the wolf didn't want to leave his own home. The dog was not happy because he knew his friend would be hungry but there wasn't anything he could do for him.*

**Evaluation:** This response attempts to address the question but there are mistakes. The wolf and the dog are not friends in the story. There is also no indication that the writer understands that the wolf is making a decision based on his fear of losing his freedom. The writer shows little insight into the motivation of the characters.

**Question 6—Score 3 Response:** *In this story the dog and the wolf both want to be well fed and taken care of. The wolf thinks that the dog has the best life so he goes with him but then the wolf thinks that his life is better so he goes back. The dog thinks that being chained up all day is all right because he can be free in the night. The wolf doesn't want to ever be chained up so he goes back to his house.*

*The dog really likes his master and he likes being fed from the table. The wolf thinks he will like that too, but then he decides he won't. Both animals make a choice. The dog decides to go home and the wolf decides to go back to his home, not to the dog's house.*

**Evaluation:** This response shows that the writer understood the important decision in the story, which was that the wolf decided to go back to his own way of life. But the writer is not clear in establishing that the wolf has chosen freedom over being well fed and cared for, which is the lesson of the story. Most of the answer is on task but it misses a major point.

**Question 6—Score 4 Response:** *The wolf wanted to be fed good food and he wanted to be pretty with a shiny coat but then he found out that he would have to wear a collar and a chain and he thought that he would really hate that. So he decided to stay where he was and let the dog go home without him.*

*The dog didn't really decide anything because he always was wearing a collar and chain. He thought that it was all right because he was treated good and he liked his life. When the wolf left him, the dog didn't understand why the wolf made the choice he did. The dog would never choose to be hungry even if he had to wear a chain.*

*I think if you don't know any better then sometimes you just do things that you think are okay. The dog didn't know any better, but the wolf did.*

**Evaluation:** This response shows that the writer clearly understood the question and clearly understood the nature of the choices made in the passage. The piece is on topic and clearly focused. It demonstrates the writer's insight into the wolf's decision and the dog's. The ideas are all connected to each other and to the text itself. The last paragraph relates the story to real life.

Here are three additional possible open-ended questions for "The Dog and the Wolf" which might be used on a third or fourth grade exam. See how your child might respond.

- ▶ Explain why the wolf wanted to be like the dog.
- ▶ Explain why you think the wolf made a good or a bad choice.
- ▶ Explain why you would or would not want to be the dog or the wolf in this story.

Still another genre that is appearing on some elementary reading/writing assessments is poetry. This presents a challenge to most elementary students because poetry relies on highly figurative language and imagery and not on literal information. Students have to really stretch their imaginations. Examine the poem and the questions that follow. Can your fourth grader complete this task?

# Afternoon on a Hill

*By Edna St. Vincent Millay*

I will be the gladdest thing
    Under the sun!
I will touch a hundred flowers
    And not pick one.

I will look at cliffs and clouds
    With quiet eyes,
Watch the wind bow down the grass,
    And the grass rise.

And when lights begin to show
    Up from the town,
I will mark which must be mine,
    And then start down.

**MULTIPLE-CHOICE QUESTIONS**

1. Where is the speaker?
   a. in a big city
   b. in a ball field
   c. in a country garden
   d. in a supermarket

The correct answer is **c.** The answer is implied by references to flowers, cliffs, and clouds, all things found in nature.

2. This piece of writing is called
   a. a play.
   b. a story.
   c. a magazine article.
   d. a poem.

The correct answer is **d.** This question tests whether a student can identify a specific literary genre.

3.  When the narrator says " . . . quiet eyes . . . " it means that he or she is
    a.  in a peaceful mood.
    b.  is angry.
    c.  is unhappy.
    d.  is sad.

The correct answer is **a.** This questions measures whether a student can identify tone
and mood.

4.  When the narrator writes, "I will mark which must be mine . . . ." he or she is
    referring to
    a.  the lights on the cars.
    b.  the lights of the stars.
    c.  the lights of his house.
    d.  the lights of a shopping center.

The correct answer is **c.** The question tests a student's ability to interpret and predict
meaning. If the speaker is standing on a hill overlooking a city, then he or she is probably watching the lights go on in the houses below him or her and when he or she says,
"Which must be mine," he or she is probably referring to his or her own home.

5.  The word "gladdest" in the first line means
    a.  saddest.
    b.  loneliest.
    c.  happiest.
    d.  angriest.

The correct answer is **c.** This question determines a student's ability to determine
vocabulary meaning in context.

**OPEN-ENDED QUESTION**

An open-ended question for this passage might be:

6.  Tell about a time when you felt happy and peaceful.

See how your child does!

In some states there is a separate writing test for grades five or six. These separate writing exams are usually two stand-alone prompts designed to measure an elementary student's ability to generate text on his or her own, independent of a reading passage or a picture to provide inspiration. Like the high school and middle school stand-alones, these elementary stand-alones are meant to be full length pieces of writing that are fully developed and that demonstrate that the author can produce a well-organized, well-supported, and well-written essay in a timed circumstance.

Topics for these stand-alone prompts at the elementary level are always narrative and expository; persuasive writing is *not* required for this grade range. Sample topics for *narration* might be:

- ▶ Tell about the time you were on a magic carpet.
- ▶ Tell about a special day.
- ▶ Tell the story of your happiest holiday.
- ▶ Tell about a time when you were proud, happy, sad, or brave.
- ▶ Tell the story of how you met your best friend.
- ▶ Tell about a time when you had to make a choice.

Notice that narrative prompts ask the student to "tell about a time" or "tell the story of." Elementary students are expected to be familiar with the conventions of storytelling, such as plot, characterization, and conflict. They are expected to understand chronological order. They have also been introduced to certain literary conventions such as exaggeration, comparison/contrast, similes, and metaphors. They might not be expected to define the literary elements this precisely, but they should be familiar with the patterns of good narration.

Before you look at possible answers, look at the rubric that could be used to rate fifth grade responses. Remember, this is to be a full length piece of *student generated text*, which means that the piece will be rated more stringently than text based open-ended responses that are measuring the student's reading comprehension as much as his or her ability to produce original writing.

The rubric to measure this kind of writing might look like the following chart:

| SCORE | 4 | 3 | 2 | 1 |
|---|---|---|---|---|
| CONTENT | Student demonstrates creativity and imagination in responding to the task. Has a clear sense of narrative purpose with beginning, middle, and end. Includes characterization and plot. | Student demonstrates some creativity in responding to the task. Has a sense of narrative purpose with beginning, middle, and end. Characterization and plot may be limited. | Student responds to the task. Narrative purpose is uncertain. Little attention to characterization or plot. | Limited understanding of the task. No sense of narrative purpose. |
| ORGANIZATION | Student has a clear organization pattern. Paragraphs are developed. Supporting details are evident. | Student has an organization pattern. Some paragraph development. Some supporting details. | Student has unclear organizational pattern. Little or no paragraph development. Few supporting details. | Student has no organization pattern. No paragraph development. No supporting details. |
| STYLE | Student demonstrates creativity in language use and sentence variety. | Student demonstrates good use of language with some sentence variety. | Student demonstrates adequate use of language with limited sentence variety. | Student demonstrates poor use of language and no sentence variety. |
| MECHANICS | Student has no errors in spelling, punctuation, capitalization, and use of quotation marks. | Student has some errors in spelling, punctuation, capitalization, and use of quotation marks. | Student has some errors in spelling, punctuation, capitalization, and use of quotation marks. | Student has many errors in spelling, punctuation, capitalization, and use of quotation marks. |

One morning you woke up and stepped out of bed onto your carpet. Suddenly, the carpet moved under your feet and you were flying out of your bedroom window! Tell about the time you spent on your magic carpet. Where did you go? What did you see? Who did you meet?

**STAND-ALONE WRITING SAMPLE RESPONSES**

**Sample Response—Score 0:** *me go sky fly to place frend came with dog too.*

**Evaluation:** All scoring instruments indicate that zero points are reserved for totally illegible or illogical pieces; blank papers also score a zero.

**Sample Response—Score 1:** *I went to my friends house he has a magic carpet that plays songs and we watch tv all day. His mother makes us popcorn and we play fight and then we go ride bikes and I want to stay over for dinner but my mom comes home.*

*When tomorrow comes we will go to disney and have fun on the magic carpet. I take my friend with me.*

**Evaluation:** This piece has no story development. The details provided have no connection to the text and have no logical pattern of organization. Mechanics interfere with communication.

**Sample Response—Score 2:** *I was on a carpet that flew out my window and I felt really scared. We flew all around we couldn't stop. My friends house was under me and I screamed for him to come and jump on the rug. He landed and we kept going till we reached a giant's house and when my friend jumped on he hurt his foot so we soaked it in warm water like my mother tells me to do.*

*I robbed the giant and he was mad so me and my friend ran and ran all the way home.*

**Evaluation:** Although there is an attempt to develop a story, this piece rambles on in a very disjointed and fragmented way. The temporal point of view is off and mechanics are flawed; there are sentence and spelling errors.

**Sample Response—Score 3:** *One day a magic carpet was in my room when I got up. It moved back and forth and then before I could jump off it flew out the window into the sky. I was scared because it was going fast and I didn't know where I was going. Then we landed on an island and pirates were there. I was scared. The pirate king said why are you on my island and I said I want to go home. So the pirate king looked all around and he saw I had no one to help me he called a genie from off his ship and he told her to take me back home.*

*I came home and closed my window and pushed the rug under the bed. My mother wanted to know where I was and I told her I went to my friends house because I knew she wouldn't believe me if I told her. I hope she never makes me put that rug back out on my floor.*

**Evaluation:** There is a clear attempt to make up a story about the rug. The writer creates a beginning, middle, and end, but the story lacks details about characterization and plot. There is some sentence variety.

**Sample Response—Score 4:** *One morning after my alarm clock went off and my mother kept calling my name from the kitchen I woke up and my carpet was moving. I was really surprised and really scared. I said, "Where am I going and who are you?" Suddenly, a genie came out of a bottle and she said, "I am your friend and we are going to have an adventure."*

*The next thing I knew we were flying through the sky and I could see my friend's house and my school and then I saw we were flying up into the mountains. I was stuck like glue to the side of the carpet because I was holding on so tight. I didn't want to fall off. Then we landed and we were in a beautiful castle in the sky. I looked around for the genie but she was gone. Instead I heard very loud footsteps and a giant appeared.*

*The giant said, "My name is Mofesto and I am a magician and I am going to teach you magic tricks." Mofesto taught me how to do two magic tricks and when we were finished he said, "Now you can go home and show your friends." The genie came back and before we got on the carpet we had a snack together. We ate ice cream sandwiches and drank sodas and then we got back on the carpet. We flew home and the next thing I knew my mother was shaking me and shaking me. She said, "Hurry up and get dressed. You're going to be late for school. Why didn't you wake up?"*

*I was dreaming the whole time but I also knew a card trick I never knew before. Was there really no Mofesto?*

**Evaluation:** This is a very well constructed narrative that has a beginning, middle, and end with a clearly developed story. The introduction of dialogue correctly uses quotation marks and characters (genie and Mofesto) and indicates a sense of story. The writer's question about dreaming or waking indicates creativity. The use of language is excellent, including the simile, "stuck like glue." The question at the end suggests that this fifth grader probably knew the work of children's author Chris Van Allsburg, who always has a surprise ending!

Now let's take a look at a possible *expository* prompt. Another way to define expository writing is to call it writing to explain. Prompts might look like this:

- ▶ Explain why school field trips are important.
- ▶ Explain why you like to play sports.
- ▶ Explain why school is important to you.
- ▶ Tell about your favorite movie and explain why it is your favorite.

The rubric to measure this kind of writing might look like the chart on the following page:

| SCORE | 4 | 3 | 2 | 1 |
|---|---|---|---|---|
| CONTENT | Student understands the task and provides a creative and imaginative example and explanation appropriate to the topic. | Student understands the task and uses an appropriate example and explanation. | Student minimally understands the task but doesn't stay on one topic or provides a fragmented explanation. | Student does not fully address the topic. Digresses and does not use full examples. |
| FOCUS | Fully develops the topic with supporting details appropriate to the topic. | Develops the topic with supporting details appropriate to the topic. | Strays from the topic and provides few, if any, supporting details. | Has little sense of topic and provides no supporting details. |
| STYLE | Excellent use of vocabulary; sentence variety. | Good use of vocabulary; some sentence variety. | Weak vocabulary; no sentence variety. | Poor or inappropriate vocabulary; errors in sentences. |
| MECHANICS | No errors. | Few errors. | Few errors. | Errors interfere with communication. |

You have been asked to write a letter to your teacher explaining why school is important to you. You must give two reasons why school is important to you and then you must explain each one.

(Note: Students do not have to use proper letter format. The direction to write to the teacher is used to provide a sense of audience for the child.)

**EXPOSITORY WRITING SAMPLE RESPONSES**

**Sample Response—Score 0:** *school is hard and fun like the bithday today we had cupcake and milk but no lunch so I was hungery and I had no coat to go out for reces and I want to play litle lege tonite but mayber icant.*

**Evaluation:** A zero score means that the student has not responded to the task at all. Frequently, this is a serious indication of learning difficulties.

**Sample Response—Score 1:** *I like school. I have fun everyday with my friends. I go on the school bus and one day this kid had a fight and got beat up and the driver got mad so now he doesn't allow to ride the bus. His mother take him to school and then he walks home and my mother would kill me if I didn't go to school.*

*I want to learn stuff and be smart so I need to ride the bus and not get into fights with other kids.*

**Evaluation:** This response doesn't answer the task and fails to establish two reasons for the importance of schol. The piece is not organized and does not have sentence structure or varied vocabulary.

**Sample Response—Score 2:**

*Dear Ms. Smith,*

*School is important because I learn new things and I see my friends. We like to play at recess. We have a football game everyday we go outside. We are in a battle with another team. We will win because we are better. If I didn't go to school I couldn't have this much to do.*

*My mother says school is important and I believe her. She is a nurse and she is smart and my dad know this too. My mom got this award for being smart. She knows a lot of stuff about how to eat and do good things. I want to be just like her when I get big.*

**Evaluation:** Although this answer attempts to address the topic of school importance, and even though it does provide two reasons, it drifts from the topic and digresses.

The writer attempts to point out that he or she thinks school is important because of his or her mother's influence, but he or she does not complete the thought. Sentence structure is not varied and vocabulary is weak.

**Sample Response—Score 3:**

*Dear Ms. Smith,*

*School is important to me. I learn how to do things like read and know science and social studies. If I don't learn things like this now I might not get a good job when I grow up. I think that school is important. We get to learn about current events. When important things happen in the newspaper my teacher makes us talk about it and then we use the map to find new places and then learn about how the people live there. This is really fun.*

*I think school is important because kids need to learn how to be nice to each other. My friend got into trouble because he pushed a girl on the bus and he got detention. If he didn't learn from that lesson then he might grown up to be a really bad person.*

*I like school and I know it is important for me.*

**Evaluation:** This is a complete answer that demonstrates that the writer understood the task. It provides two reasons why school is important, and it gives two examples to support it. There is some digression and the vocabulary and sentence structure is grade appropriate.

**Sample Response—Score 4:**

*Dear Ms. Smith,*

*School is very important to me because I need to learn important things so I can be a famous person some day. I want to go to work and make lots of money and help people like my daddy. He is a workman for airplanes and when he doesn't do his job making sure that the airplanes are safe people could die. He always tells me that if he didn't go to school he couldn't help people and so I have to go to school to be smart just like him. Someday I want to be an engineer like my dad and I know I have to go to school and learn a lot of math and science. I like math and science, especially when the teacher gives us problems to solve because I know they make me smart.*

*I also like school because I have lots of friends I see every day. If I didn't go to school I wouldn't have fun. I'd be bored a lot. Because I have a lot of friends in school I get to be the class monitor and that makes me feel important. So school is very important because of these two things.*

**Evaluation:** This answer clearly identifies the importance of school for the writer and it gives two reasons why school is important. The sentences are varied and the vocabulary choice is excellent. The author introduces a father as a role model and then goes on to talk about math and science as favorite subjects. The last paragraph is particularly insightful because it addresses the important social skills learned in school.

## Elementary Testing and the *No Child Left Behind Act*

ELEMENTARY TESTING IS extremely important for schoolchildren. It is an important opportunity to evaluate performance and determine possible special learning needs. In other words, if your child falls seriously below the guidelines considered to be grade level, then further testing for learning disabilities may be required. Generally, on the four-point scale, the "2" range is considered minimum competency, or even borderline grade level.

Standards based testing is in no small way driven by the need to identify the individual learning needs of children. If your child is a below grade level reader in grade three, then without help, his or her learning will be compromised in every subject for the rest of his educational experience.

But what does *help* mean? Not all children who fall below competency ranges on tests will require testing for learning disabilities or other special needs. Remediation in the form of one-on-one tutoring, or a special small group reading class, may be what is needed. Most states are building into their new testing regimes the requirement that all children who fall below state minimum competency guidelines be provided with such remediation—at the school district's expense. Some parents also choose private help from private sources such as Sylvan Learning Centers. Of course, this comes at a price.

Whatever the provisions for help, as your child progresses through school, it becomes more and more important for you to know just what is expected of students and how your child measures up against his or her peers.

It is important at this point to remind you that by the school year 2005–2006, schools throughout the country will be required to test students in reading and mathematics *every* year from grade three through to grade eight. Currently, that is not the case in most states. But as standards-based assessment moves along, states will add tests each year, and it is hoped that those tests will be one way to be sure that none of America's children are left behind.

# Looking at Elementary School Exams: Mathematics

**Perhaps one** of the most serious inadequacies of public school instruction in the past 20 years has been its failure to expect students to acquire mathematics skills beyond basic competency. Students have been permitted to take basic skills math or minimum competency math as high school graduation requirements only to find themselves taking remedial math classes in college. Poor math skills also find students unable to land other than minimum wage employment. Just as it is impossible to function without reading and writing skills, it is impossible to compete in an increasingly technological marketplace with only borderline mathematics skills.

American business has been forced to provide expensive on the job training to compensate for the deficiencies of these virtually unskilled workers, and it did not take long for American businesses to move outside the United States to find the same skill levels in foreign workers for half the wages they had to pay young Americans. So the road to raising expectations, whether in Language Arts or mathematics, has been paved by a variety of needs, not the least of which was business.

Public education has heeded this rallying cry, and one of its first steps was to raise the mathematics requirements for high school graduates. In short, no more "easy" math. Just as the reading passages are longer and more complex, so are the math problems. And just as you have to build strengths from kindergarten through grade twelve in English/Language Arts, so, too, does a mathematics program have to build from one grade level to the next.

In elementary classrooms across the country, students are challenged daily with math, which doesn't always look like math. Manipulatives have made numbers and problem solving both accessible and fun. Problem solving which centers around everyday experiences such as measuring the playground, maintaining records for a school store, even calculating the percentage of students wearing sneakers as opposed to boots or shoes, becomes part of classroom mathematics. Kids as young as five or six are doing data analysis and probability—it's just not called that. The complexity of the mathematical tasks increases, but the basic foundations for complex math are laid in kindergarten.

The state of Washington has an excellent website, easily used by students, parents, and educators. It contains dozens of math practice problems by grade level, K-6, in all of the categories tested. It provides an excellent way to see just how the categories and skill strands move in complexity from one grade to the next (www.k12.wa.us/toolkits).

Let's look at sample problems for grade three in these four categories:

1. Number Sense and Concepts
2. Spatial Sense and Geometry
3. Data Analysis, Probability and Statistics, and Discrete Mathematics
4. Patterns, Functions, and Algebra

1. Which of the following is NOT true?
    a. $2 \times 3 = 3 \times 2$
    b. $2 + 3 = 3 - 2$
    c. $3 + 4 = 4 + 3$
    d. $3 \times 4 = 4 \times 3$

The correct answer is **b.** Choices **a, b,** and **c** are all true. Choice **b** is NOT true, so it is the right answer.

This question requires a third grader to apply the commutative property. At this level, most states do not require students to *know* that they are applying the commutative property, but students are required to *understand* this number concept.

2. Athena vacuums every Friday and gets paid $2. How many weeks must she vacuum in order to earn enough money to earn $10?
    a. 2
    b. 3
    c. 4
    d. 5

The correct answer is **d.** After 1 week she has $2, after 2 weeks she has $4, after 3 weeks she has $6, after 4 weeks she has $8, and after 5 weeks she has $10. The answer is 5 weeks.

This question requires the elementary student to use logical thinking and to be able to count by twos. Note that an adult might just calculate an answer by using $10 \div 2$. Your child will not learn division until fourth grade. In third grade, a child solves this question counting by twos.

3. Which answer choice contains only even numbers?
    a. 42, 5, 16, 10
    b. 8, 6, 12, 7
    c. 22, 10, 42, 56
    d. 18, 19, 28, 90

The correct answer is **c.** The even numbers are 0, 2, 4, 6, 8, and so on. All even numbers end in 0, 2, 4, 6, or 8.

This question requires that a student is familiar with the terminology of odd and even. A third grader should be able to tell the difference between an odd number and an even number.

**4.** What does the 5 in the number 522 mean?

    **a.**  5 ones

    **b.**  5 tens

    **c.**  5 hundreds

    **d.**  none of the above

The correct answer is **c.** The 5 is in the hundreds place and it means 5 hundreds.

Third graders learn place value up to the thousands place in most states. In many schools, children use manipulatives (small cubes) to visualize 1, 10, 100, and 1,000. Visual representation of place value is also common in this grade. For example, the ones are represented by a drawing of a square. The tens, by a stack of 10 squares. The hundreds by 10 rows of 10 squares. And the thousands would be represented by a 3-D diagram of a large cube divided into 10 by 10 smaller cubes.

### SPATIAL SENSE AND GEOMETRY FOR GRADE THREE

**1.** Which 2 triangles below are congruent?

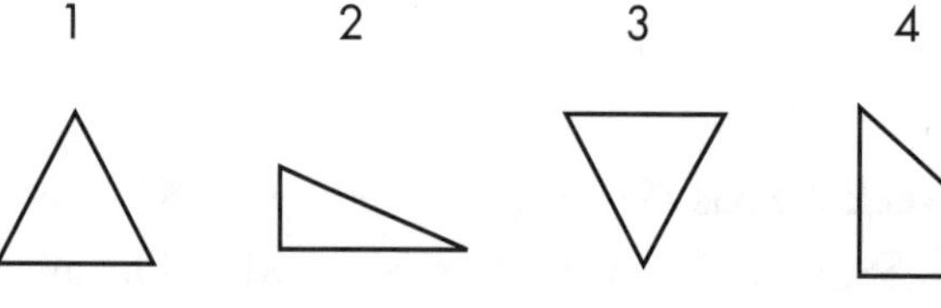


    **a.**  2 and 4

    **b.**  1 and 3

    **c.**  2 and 3

    **d.**  1 and 4

The correct answer is **b.** Congruent means *the same*. Here triangles 1 and 3 are the same.

This question tests terminology. Not all states will require third graders to know what congruent means, but most require this knowledge by fourth grade.

**2.** What time is it on the clock below?

    **a.** almost 2 o'clock

    **b.** almost 1 o'clock

    **c.** almost 12 o'clock

    **d.** almost 11 o'clock

The correct answer is **c.** The small hand is on the 12 and the larger hand is approaching the 12. This means that it is almost 12 o'clock.

Third graders are expected to be able to tell time.

**3.** Below is a picture of Helen's garden. What is the perimeter of Helen's garden?

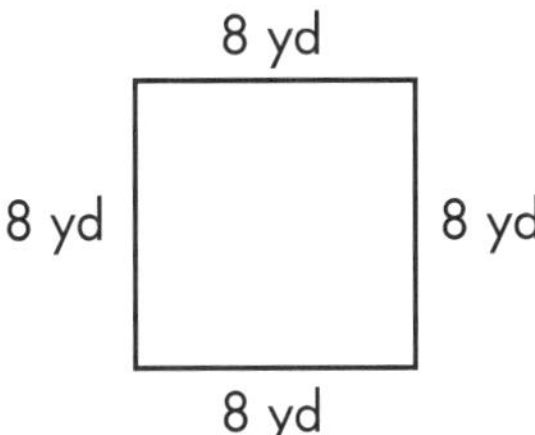


    **a.** 8 yards

    **b.** 16 yards

    **c.** 32 yards

    **d.** 64 yards

The correct answer is **c.** The perimeter of her yard is the distance around her yard. Here the distance around the square yard is 8 + 8 + 8 + 8. This equals 32 yards.

This question requires the third grader to apply the geometry concept of perimeter in a simple real-world scenario.

**4.** Mr. Brown's class planted flowers outside of their classroom. Victoria filled a watering can with water for the flowers. What unit would be best to use if Victoria wanted to measure how much water was in the pail?

   **a.** centimeters

   **b.** pounds

   **c.** cups

   **d.** inches

The correct answer is **c.** The amount of fluid (water) would be measured in cups. Centimeters and inches measure lengths. Pounds measure weight.

This question gives a third grader a "real-world" example of the application of the different units of measurement.

### DATA ANALYSIS, PROBABILITY AND STATISTICS, AND DISCRETE MATHEMATICS

**1.** The third grade teachers made a chart of how many students they have. Whose class has the least number of students?

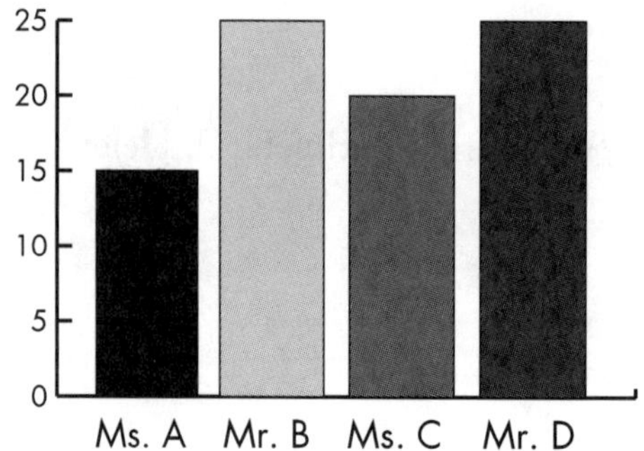


   **a.** Ms. A's class

   **b.** Mr. B's class

   **c.** Ms. C's class

   **d.** Mr. D's class

The correct answer is **a.** The bar for Ms. A's class is shortest, so Ms. A's class has the least number of students.

This question requires your third grader to interpret data in a real-world scenario. In classrooms all across the country, students are constructing bar graphs as early as kindergarten. For example, a teacher may make a "Birthday Graph" to show how many students in the class have birthdays in each of the 12 months.

2. Each ♥ represents 2 valentines in the pictograph below. How many valentines did Emily get?

| Student | Valentines |
| --- | --- |
| Gregory | ♥ ♥ |
| Emily | ♥ ♥ ♥ ♥ |
| Amanda | ♥ ♥ ♥ ♥ ♥ ♥ ♥ |
| Sammy | ♥ ♥ ♥ |

   **a.** 4
   **b.** 7
   **c.** 8
   **d.** 10

The correct answer is **c.** The table shows 4 hearts next to Emily. Each heart = 2 valentines. Emily got $4 \times 2 = 8$ valentines.

This question requires the student to use data from a pictograph.

3. There are 6 stickers in a bag. 1 is a cat sticker, 1 is a dog sticker, 1 is a bunny sticker, and 3 are butterfly stickers. If Jane reaches into the bag, which sticker will she most likely get?

   **a.** cat
   **b.** dog
   **c.** bunny
   **d.** butterfly

The correct answer is **d.** There are 3 butterfly stickers in the bag. There are only 1 of the other kinds in the bag. Jane will most likely pick a butterfly sticker.

This question requires students to think in terms of probability. Your third grader probably won't think "Ooh, a probability question!" when he or she reads this, but mathematical reasoning should lead your child to pick the right answer. Students calculate odds in fourth grade.

**4.** Mrs. Powell keeps track of how many turns each student gets on the computer by making a chart. Below is Mrs. Powell's chart. Which student had the most turns?

| Student Name | Number of Turns on Computer |
|---|---|
| Amy | 13 |
| Derrick | 18 |
| Richard | 15 |
| Sean | 19 |
| Warren | 14 |

   **a.** Amy

   **b.** Derrick

   **c.** Sean

   **d.** Richard

The correct answer is **c.** Sean had 19 turns. This number is more than any of the other students.

This question requires a third grader to read data from a table. The data is presented in a real-world scenario relative to data your child may be collecting in school.

PATTERNS, FUNCTIONS AND ALGEBRA

**1.** Which pattern below follows the same pattern as **ABCABCABC**?

   **a.** ♈♈☺♈♈☺♈♈☺

   **b.** □△✪□△✪□△✪

   **c.** ◆✤◆✤◆✤◆✤

   **d.** ✿✾✾✿✾✾✿✾✾

The correct answer is **b.** Choice **b** is the only choice that contains an ABC pattern. ABC patterns have 3 things that repeat over and over.

These days children learn about "AB patterns" in kindergarten. For example, your child may have made a work of art that followed this pattern. As the years progress, students learn ABB and ABC patterns. The pattern SQUARE, TRIANGLE, SUN is simply an ABC pattern.

**2.** What is the rule for the In-Out table below?

| IN | OUT |
| --- | --- |
| 2 | 5 |
| 5 | 8 |
| 9 | 12 |

    **a.** add 1 to the **IN** number

    **b.** add 2 to the **IN** number

    **c.** add 3 to the **IN** number

    **d.** add 4 to the **IN** number

The correct answer is **c.** You can solve this question by finding out which answer makes sense. Adding 3 to the IN number will give you the OUT number.

IN-OUT tables are presented to third graders as a means to provide a foundation for algebra they will encounter in the future. Sometimes a fictional "machine" is presented to these young students with one number going IN and another coming OUT. The child can then reason: "What did the magical machine do to change the IN number into the OUT number?" At this level, only simple operations (plus and minus) are presented in IN-OUT tables or IN-OUT machines.

**3.** There are 3 girls and 4 boys at the bus stop. Which choice shows how to find the total number of children at the bus stop?

    **a.** $4 - 3$

    **b.** $4 \times 3$

    **c.** $3 + 4$

    **d.** $3 \times 4$

The correct answer is **c.** To find the total you just add the girls plus the boys. This is 3 + 4.

These types of questions also serve as a foundation for algebra. This can be classified as algebraic thinking. Here the student knows how many boys and girls there are, but he or she arrives at the answer by realizing that the number of girls needs to be added to the number of boys in order to find the total. This is algebraic thinking. In fourth grade this idea is expanded. The same question may add a variable, $T$ for total, and the answer would be $T = 3 + 4$. Other times a box may be used, so $\boxed{\phantom{x}} = 3 + 4$.

4.  5 ◎ 10

   If ◎ is a number and all three numbers above are in order from smallest to biggest, what might ◎ equal?

   a.  1
   b.  3
   c.  4
   d.  6

The correct answer is **d.** The ◎ must be a number between 5 and 10. Of the choices, only 6 is between 5 and 10.

This question uses an image, the ◎, to represent a number. In other words, this is third grade algebra.

And now let's see what the standards might look like for fourth grade.

## Grade Four Mathematics Assessments

THE BIGGEST DIFFERENCE between grade three and grade four mathematics is the amount of terminology that your child needs to know and understand. For example, your child is expected to recognize parallel lines and perpendicular lines; equilateral triangles, isosceles triangles, and scalene triangles; average (mean), median, and mode; radius verses diameter; simple ratios and percents; and right, acute, and obtuse angles. Word problems incorporate more information and require long division. Number patterns are trickier. Your child should be able to relate quarter turns, half turns, and so forth to degree measures. Three-dimensional solids are tested with the assumption that your child knows a face from an edge from a vertex. Slides are now called translations; turns are rotations; and flips are reflections. There is a lot to know when it comes to fourth grade math terminology. Most adults are left scratching their heads when they hear these terms! Let's look at some examples of fourth grade sample test questions.

### NUMBER SENSE AND CONCEPTS

The following number concepts question tests comparing decimal values by placing measurements into a table for the fourth grader to analyze. Notice that these questions are no longer as simple as biggest/smallest and highest/lowest; instead, the child is asked to find the second tallest height. This question requires the fourth grader to read and comprehend what is being asked of him or her. He or she then has to determine that he or she must compare all of the values in the second column and rank them in order to find the second highest number.

Ms. Paul's class planted sprouts while working on their plants unit. Five students measured their sprouts with a ruler.

| Student | Sprout Height |
| --- | --- |
| Aaron | .05 m |
| Bethie | .12 m |
| Carl | .09 m |
| Danny | .07 m |
| Edgar | .06 m |

Which student measured the second tallest sprout?
   a. Aaron
   b. Bethie
   c. Carl
   d. Danny

The correct answer is **c**. The tallest sprout was measured by Bethie and was .12 m. The next tallest sprout was measured by Carl and was .09 m.


### SPATIAL SENSE AND GEOMETRY

This geometry question tests the fourth grade child's knowledge of 3-D figure terminology. It also requires him or her to visualize the figure shown as a 3-D object, mentally accounting for its 3-D shape and attributes.

The object below is a rectangular solid.

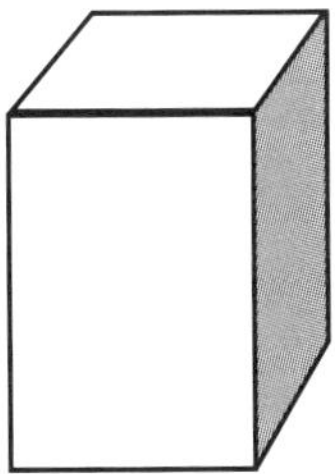

Which of the following statements about the object is true?
   a. the object has 4 faces
   b. the object has 4 vertices
   c. the object has 6 faces
   d. the object has 6 vertices

The correct answer is **c.** A vertex (plural *vertices*) is where 2 line segments meet. Pick up a shoebox and count the vertices with your child. A rectangular solid and a cube both have 8 vertices. The faces are the flat surfaces that are joined at the edges to form the 3-D object. Again, examine a shoebox and count the faces. A rectangular solid and a cube both have 6 faces.

### DATA ANALYSIS, PROBABILITY AND STATISTICS, AND DISCRETE MATH

This probability and statistics question tests the fourth grader's ability to correctly calculate the odds based on a simple real-world scenario.

> Megan places 9 gumdrops in a bag. 2 are red, 1 is yellow, 3 are green, 1 is orange, and 2 are purple. If Lauren reaches into the bag, what is the probability that she will pull out a red gumdrop?
>
> **a.** $\frac{1}{3}$
>
> **b.** $\frac{2}{9}$
>
> **c.** $\frac{1}{9}$
>
> **d.** $\frac{2}{3}$

The correct answer is **b.** There are 9 gumdrops in all. Only 2 are red. So the probability of picking a red gumdrop is 2 out of 9. This is written as $\frac{2}{9}$.

### PATTERNS, FUNCTIONS, AND ALGEBRA

This algebra question turns the IN-OUT table into an *x-y* table. Note that the child must be able to figure out the "rule" and apply it in order to calculate the value of ♠.

Which statement about the table shown below is true?

| x | y |
|---|---|
| 1 | 4 |
| 3 | 7 |
| 5 | ♠ |
| 7 | 11 |

**a.** The rule is *x* times 4 equals *y*.

**b.** ♠ is equal to 20.

**c.** The rule is *x* plus 3 equals *y*.

**d.** ♠ is equal to 9.

The correct answer is **d.** If you look at the chart, you will see that the rule is "$x$ plus 4 equals $y$." If you need ideas to see what the rule might be, you should look at the answer choices. If you take $x = 5$ and apply the "$x$ plus 4 equals $y$" rule, you get $5 + 4$ equals $y$. Since $5 + 4 = 9$, $y = 9$.

The questions that measure elementary math vary from state to state. Some tests rely solely on multiple choice. Most new tests incorporate the short answer and the extended response which require youngsters to show their calculations and/or explain their thinking. In some states, math tools such as calculators and rulers are permitted for the entire test. In some states they are permitted for parts of the test.

Once again, it is important that you visit your state's website to know exactly what your state requires. Appendix A provides the site addresses with some simple instructions for you to follow.

CHAPTER

# Bringing It All Together

**All that** glitters is not gold. It's an old saying, but it can be applied to the testing movement in education today. It may all sound good, and it may well prove to be good, but for right now the jury is out. There are educators who say that underneath the glitter of all that testing is lead! Opponents of standards based testing argue that all this testing detracts from classroom instruction in other content areas, diverts valuable resources away from more pressing problems, handicaps real teacher creativity, limits student engagement rather than promotes it, and ultimately punishes rather than assists the very people it was designed to help in the first place.

Let's look at some of the arguments. You can be the judge.

Let's start with *teaching to the tests*. Does this entire high stakes testing trend mean that teachers are going to drill only for those subjects which are tested? Will the pressure for student performance in reading and math drive teachers to throw away precious time for social studies, science, health, geography, music, art, and technology instruction in order to be able to teach only what is tested? This is a very important question and one that has not escaped the attention of the major educational organizations, schools of education, and research institutes.

It makes sense, say the skeptics. If a teacher fears that a particular test instrument will judge his or her students' performance, then why wouldn't he or she gear students up for that instrument? And make no mistake; teachers *are* being held accountable for test results. Remember those report cards we talked about? On some state report cards, school districts are being told to post the school's test results *and* to report results by teacher. Even if the state doesn't require such public posting, every teacher knows that the building principal has that information. It will become part of the teacher's overall evaluation, not to mention part of the next parent association meeting's agenda. Such accountability may become the basis for merit pay, which is a highly controversial means of identifying teachers who are successful. But successful at what?

Critics of the new legislation to test every grade every year in reading and math worry that teachers will abandon instruction in social studies, science, and health, to name just three content areas. Most elementary classroom teachers will tell you that there aren't enough hours in the day to accomplish an already overwhelming curriculum that includes character (values) education, dental health week, national book week, President's week, bicycle safety, fire safety, anti-smoking and anti-drug programs, not to mention the art, music, and foreign language programs that are so critical in an elementary classroom.

Secondary educators will tell you that they are trying to bolster academic performance in students who are holding down full-time jobs, confronting parenting issues of their own, and dealing with social issues that even their adult counterparts can't imagine overcoming.

And are they wrong? If testing attention is turned to the basics, and no one can argue that reading, writing, and math are not the basics, then aren't classroom teachers simply following the lead of their government? If the Congress of the United States has declared that reading, writing, and math are the benchmarks of a sound education, then what else would we have elementary teachers teach and secondary teachers emphasize? Teachers will have to sacrifice the other content areas to find the time to be sure their students pass the exit exams. Their students' promotions to the next grade level, whether or not they will need remediation, and high school graduation depends on them.

But how can we argue with social studies educators who fear that limited resources, both time and money, will be diverted from their programs? Isn't studying history and geography critical in promoting the kind of citizenship required to take our nation into the twenty-first century? Haven't we been told over and over again that without global consciousness, multicultural sensitivity, and understanding our place as a world leader is in jeopardy? And how about promoting more active citizenship? Shouldn't we be working harder to promote community participation and developing a more informed electorate? How do you do that if all your attention is on reading and math?

Here are two possible, positive answers. First, if classroom teachers integrate reading, writing, and math into social studies and science, to name just two, then can't more than one goal be accomplished? The answer to that question is, "Yes, but . . . " Traditional teaching methods don't always lend themselves to such integration, and although the current generation of teachers entering our classrooms has been trained in newer methodologies, many veteran teachers have not. And, despite the movement toward block scheduling and year-round schooling, most schools in the United States still follow a traditional school year and daily schedule. Switching to what may be more effective is costly. Teacher training is very expensive. New teaching materials are expensive.

Second, if the new accountability efforts work, then we should be promoting more competent students from the elementary program to the secondary level. Better equipped to handle the basic skills, and better disciplined as students, the secondary student of the future should be prepared to do more homework and be more independent in his or her learning. Secondary educators should not have to deal with juniors or seniors in high school who are unable or unwilling to read their textbooks; who are unwilling and unable to do research. In addition, we should see better citizenship in our students. In short, with increased accountability, our children should become more academically focused and more motivated.

President Bush's agenda in reading is a return to phonics instruction. Many school systems have spent millions of dollars on reading programs which do not emphasize phonics. Where do they get the money to change all that? Should we change all that? The emphasis on phonics comes from the importance placed on scientifically proven methods of instruction. The *No Child Left Behind Act* explicitly outlines the importance of adopting programs, proven to work, based on scientific research methods. Well, the data is in on phonics. It works. But the data, albeit less scientific perhaps, is also in on the whole language approach to reading, which emphasizes whole text and more contextualized reading.

While we're busy spending more and more of our school budgets on teacher training, new text books, and reading programs, how about the research that has told us that smaller classes and one-on-one reading remediation efforts in grades K-3 will dramatically improve a student's efforts in the later grades? And what about the research that has told us that the students most in need are the ones who need social intervention, the children who need after school care because two working parents are the norm today, as is the single working mother? In high achieving schools, the need to recognize and confront the issues of homelessness and child abuse and all the vagaries of the low socioeconomic burdens on America's poorest families will not be felt at school board meetings. But in low performing schools, where the social needs are the greatest, critics see standards based tests as a double-edged sword. On the one side will be the opportunity to confront low achievement and develop plans to help those students gain momentum. On the other side will be the burden of blame and precious few resources to make a difference. Either side of the sword will require talent, commitment, and money.

Opportunity in a democratic society can almost be defined as the accessibility of all its citizens to education. What nobler goal would there be than to use standards based tests to mirror performance and demand better? But it is also a dangerous way to point the finger at schools, communities, and children who are struggling to overcome obstacles far greater than phonics and computation strategies.

Educators fear that testing will be used to punish low achieving schools and that help, in the form of funding, will be unavailable. All the talent and dedication in the world cannot reduce class size or provide teacher training. All the effective leadership of principals cannot produce the resources needed to recruit new teachers, fund before- and after-school homework programs, or provide additional social workers to help the growing ranks of homeless children in our nation's classrooms.

The issue of the tests themselves needs addressing, too. Remember that each of the fifty states is developing its own unique high stakes tests based on uniquely developed standards. True, there is remarkable similarity and consistency, but there are still four states out there that are very far behind in test development. And of the fifty states, there is no guarantee that all the tests will be equally well-developed. The plus side of the test issue is that there will be a nationally developed test given in grades four and eight. The National Assessment of Education Progress (NAEP) will be a national barometer for states to use to measure their individual state results. But the downside of the NAEP program is that parents must be notified when the tests are to be given, and they have the right to remove their children from testing. This may seriously compromise the validity of the NAEP.

Where do you fit into all of this? What can you do to help your child? First and foremost, you must be knowledgeable.


## Understand Your State's Requirements

FIRST, VISIT YOUR child's principal and tell him or her that you are interested in knowing more about your state's testing program. Ask for whatever material he or she may have for you to look at.

Second, visit your state education department's website listed in Appendix A. Plan to spend some time just browsing through the links. Don't hesitate to follow a link marked *For Teachers* or *For Administrators*. Be sure to look for links labeled *Assessment* or *Eval-*

*uation.* Go to *Curriculum and Instruction* and look for *Standards* and *Curriculum Content.* Don't hesitate to go back to the principal if you need help navigating the site or if you need clarification about something you don't understand. Suggest that your parents' association have a meeting set aside just for discussion and explanation of testing in your school. Work with your parents' association to plan and publicize the meeting. Building administrators want parent involvement and nothing is more discouraging for them than having information, planning a meeting, making the coffee, and having no audience.

Third, contact your child's teacher and set up a parent-teacher meeting to discuss your child's specific progress towards your state's testing goals. Ask what the teacher is doing to promote the state standards. Ask to see samples of your child's work that indicate how he or she is progressing towards the standards.

Fourth, make school and learning part of your everyday conversation at home. If you have obtained test questions from the state website or a practice test from the building administrator, try to go over some practice questions with your child.

Fifth, encourage reading, reading, and more reading. Turn off the TV!

## Does Your Child's School Reflect the New Standards?

ARE THERE LOADS of student work on display in the halls and on the classroom walls? Student writing should be everywhere. A school that honors its students' work honors its students.

Are the classrooms busy with students at various activities or is the teacher monitoring students working silently at their desks? The new standards encourage children to be actively engaged in learning. That means that the teacher should not be the only one talking. The kids should be busy and collaborating with one another as they work.

Are the principal and assistant principal always in their offices when you visit, or do you find them out visiting classrooms or walking the halls? An effective building leader knows what's going on all the time. He or she is eager to watch students learning or performing. They read the work hanging on the walls. They know their children by name.

Does your child's school have a well-stocked library? Does your child bring books home from the library? Does his or her class visit the library?

Does your school have a cultural arts agenda? Do students have the opportunity to go to assemblies and listen to or see speakers or performers? Listening is a skill included on many state tests and the ability to listen to a speaker for an extended period of time is important practice.

Are parents like you invited to help in the classroom? At the elementary level, parent participation is a given. By middle school, and certainly high school, it's a given that parents stay home and send the kids to school. But try to change that. Offer to help a particular teacher. Offer to help the librarian. Volunteer to go on field trips. If there is a special program at the school, ask if you can attend. Nothing speaks more loudly to your child than your active participation in his or her school life. And nothing is more powerful than the fact that you know his or her teachers and they know you!

Do you go to school board meetings? Do you know what's in the budget and what's been cut? Participating in your school board meetings is an important way for you to find out what your district plans to do about implementing the new standards and the new testing requirements. You will find out if there are plans to hire teachers or provide remedial classes. You can voice your opinion about the importance of new textbooks or more teacher training.

Voting in school board elections and for your school district's budget is an opportunity for you to have an immediate and lasting impact in a voting process that has direct effect on your money and your family. Yet fewer and fewer people cast votes in this election. As a matter of fact, most people don't even know who their local school board members are, nor do they know what their school budgets prioritize. You need to know! If your child's school has math or reading scores that are not what you think they should be, you need to find out what will be done to help improve them. You need to know if the school board is going to cut funding for music and art to pay for athletics. You need to argue for what you believe should be the priorities of the schools your children attend.

## Does Your Home Reflect the New Standards?

IS YOUR HOME truly committed to educational excellence? When you ask, "What did you do in school today?" do you accept "Nothing" as the answer? Or do you ask to see schoolwork? If none comes home, or there is no homework, that is your first invitation to talk to a teacher. Your child should start having homework in first grade, and by middle school homework should be a regular part of your family's evening routine.

Do you look at the homework? Is the assignment drill and practice? In math this could be important reinforcement of math skills learned in class. But if all your child comes home with for fifth grade language arts is a spelling list to memorize or fill in the blank workbook pages, you might want to ask about the extended writing assignments he or she should be having.

When you look at graded work, is there evidence that the teacher has used a rubric to grade written work? Are there comments to suggest how the work can be improved? Ask the teacher for a copy of the rubric and keep it handy to remind your child of its importance. If you do not understand what a "4" or a "6" should look like, ask the teacher for a model paper. The purpose behind rubrics is to help students identify where there is a weakness in their writing and to help them improve. It is not enough to say, "organization was weak." A student should be shown a sample of work that is up to the highest standard.

Is your child coming home with reading and writing homework in subjects other than reading? Are social studies questions full sentence and full paragraph answers? Are those full-length answers being read and responded to by the teacher? If all your child's written homework comes back with a simple check mark, then you might want to ask the teacher about grading methods. It is unreasonable to expect that a middle school social studies teacher read and respond to 120 composition length homework assignments every night, but at least once a week, extended writing should be teacher graded.

At the high school level, how much reading and writing is expected of your child? Too many high school teachers simply give up trying to get students to complete reading assignments. Kids today are too busy with jobs and outside interests. Hopefully, as higher expectations and test requirements affect more and more students, attitudes about learning and studying will improve. Until then, are you ready to take on a reluctant fifteen-year-old who claims there "was no homework?"

Does your household value reading? Is the daily newspaper available? Are there books and magazines handy? Does your family engage in discussion about current events or community issues? Speaking and listening are two very important components of Language Arts skills, and you can easily support them at home. Listen to a television program with your children and discuss the issues presented. It doesn't have to be the History Channel or a documentary. The social issues raised on some of today's primetime television programs lend themselves to excellent discussion topics with your middle to high school student.

## Reading the State Report Card

THERE ARE TWO report cards now mandated by the new *No Child Left Behind Act*. By the academic year 2002–2003, each state must have a report card and so must each school district. Both report cards must contain essentially the same information:

- ▶ Student academic achievement on state reading and math tests disaggregated by sub-groups
  [Note: This means that your school and district must break down the percentages of students whose scores were below grade level, basic, proficient, or advanced by such categories as male and female.]
- ▶ Comparison of students at basic, proficient, and advanced levels
- ▶ Graduation rates for the high school(s) in your district
- ▶ Number and name of schools identified for improvement
- ▶ Comparison of the actual academic achievement levels for all groups of students compared to the annual objectives for such groups
- ▶ The professional qualifications of teachers
  [Note: This provision is to alert parents to the use of out of license teachers in content areas, like math, science, and foreign language. If there are shortages, teachers may be teaching these subjects without the proper certification. You should know if this is the case in your child's classroom.]
- ▶ The percentage of students not tested

The *No Child Left Behind Act* has required that this information about testing results be made public because you, as a parent, have the right to know exactly how your child, his or her school, and the district is performing against other schools and districts in your county and state. It's called accountability and wherever and whenever your parents association or school board holds its meeting to go over the report cards, you should make it your business to be there. If you don't find an invitation forthcoming, call your district office to ask where the report cards are. It's your right and your obligation to know.

There will be many different ways of presenting report card data, and you will probably need some help in figuring out what it all means. A good meeting will have the data presented and explained in such a way that you understand it. If you don't understand, ask and ask again. There is a lot riding on this information. Just as the tests have high stakes for your child, they have high stakes for teachers, administrators, and school district officials.

## ACCOUNTABILITY

The stakes for teachers: No teacher wants to have the lowest passing rate on the reading test. But no parent wants his or her child in that teacher's class either. Now, there are many factors contributing to a class's performance and teacher competence is only one. But if, for three years in a row, the same teacher has had the same poor performance, then something needs to be addressed. After the first year, perhaps some new teaching methods or a new course are in order. After the second, perhaps some peer coaching is needed. But by the third year, it may be time for a grade change. You can request information about a teacher's past record of test performance, but do it tactfully and confidentially.

The stakes for administrators: No building principal wants his or her school to have the lowest passing rate in the district or any one of the teachers to have the lowest passing rate on the reading test. A good principal wants the school, its teachers, and its children to be successful. So, just as a classroom teacher will be held accountable, so will the principal. And just like the teacher will have to make some plans to address why there is an inadequacy in the classroom, so will the building principal be forced to address that building's needs. He or she will have to come up with an improvement plan to ensure that attention is paid to improving scores next year and increasing graduation rates. That may mean introducing a new textbook, teacher training, reducing class size, or enlisting a partnership with a local college or university, just to name a few options. The *No Child Left Behind Act* allows funding for school-based initiatives to improve school performance. But if a school fails to improve over a three-year period, that is, if a school is designated a "failing school" for three consecutive years, then parents may have a school choice option.

School district officials have responsibility for big budgets and do not want to be faced with the burden of failing schools. The last thing they want is the nightmare of school choice plans and public outcry. They also don't want to have to repair failing schools with limited budgets and a failing school costs lots of money! True, the *No Child Left Behind Act* is the safety net to provide funding for reading and math programs to help bolster student performance. It makes funds available for teacher training, library development, administrative leadership, and a host of other support programs from assistance for limited English proficient students to help for homeless students, but federal funds will only help; they will not alone support school reform. If a school district has to provide expensive remediation programs, hire resource teachers, provide for new materials and supplies, reduce class size, increase funding for social services, or provide teacher training programs, then their school budgets will have to go up and they may have to raise local taxes. Then no one will be happy. It's much easier *not* to have the problem, and that brings us right back to you and your child.

Perhaps the most important piece in this puzzle of improvement is your child. The results of all this testing will have profound implications for your child's future. If your child has fallen below level, your school district must provide you with *detailed* notification that includes the specific remediation program that will be provided to serve his or her learning needs.

School district leaders know that with your help everybody wins and the stakes are high all around. So get involved today. Start with a school board meeting. Visit a website. Get to know your school district leaders. Ask questions and most important, talk to your children. Let them know you are interested and concerned. Let them know just how high the stakes really are!

# Your Guide to State Websites

**The following** websites are for each of the fifty State Education Departments. Remember, an informed parent is an asset. State, local, and classroom educators want you to have the information you need to help your child succeed.

When you enter each state website, you will be on the homepage. Follow the links designated *For Parents*. Do not hesitate to go into *Curriculum and Instruction* to find information about state standards and state benchmarks that have been adopted—by subject—for your child's grade level. You can then begin to understand what the state says your child should be learning and measure it against what he or she is actually doing in school. You can then use this information to ask informed questions of your child's classroom teacher. One especially useful tool that you will see on all state websites will be the writing rubrics used to score the writing tests. Download these rubrics and post them on the refrigerator. Your child has probably seen these in class and this is good reinforcement.

As you scan your state website, you should also follow any links labeled *Assessment*. Many states display actual past sample examinations on their sites for the express purpose of having classroom teachers and students understand exactly what will be tested and how. Look for *Sample Responses* that often provide a detailed explanation of how each paper was scored. These sample items can be used for test practice, whether at home or in the classroom.

Other important information included on your state website will be the *Report Card* for the state. Just how did your district do in comparison to other districts in the state? Some states actually let you access your individual school right from the main website. In that case you can check your school's progress. If the state website does not give your school's information, then you can obtain this information from your school district office or the building principal. These documents can be confusing to read at first, but do not hesitate to ask for help. You should know just where your school falls in its yearly testing program.

Before you begin your search, two things deserve repeating. First, an educated parent is an asset. Second, once you have information, use it productively to cooperate with your child's teacher, to encourage, and to support your child's education.

## State Departments of Education

**ALABAMA TEACHER EDUCATION AND CERTIFICATION OFFICE**

State Department of Education

50 North Ripley Street

P.O. Box 302101

Montgomery, Alabama 36104

334-242-9935

www.alsde.edu

**ALASKA DEPARTMENT OF EDUCATION**

801 West 10th Street, Suite 200

Juneau, AK 99801-1894

907-465-2800

www.educ.state.ak.us

**ARIZONA DEPARTMENT OF EDUCATION**

1535 West Jefferson Street

Phoenix, Arizona 85007

602-542-4361

800-352-4558

www.ade.state.az.us

**ARKANSAS DEPARTMENT OF EDUCATION**

Four Capitol Mall

Little Rock, AR 72201

501-682-4475

http://arkedu.state.ar.us

**CALIFORNIA DEPARTMENT OF EDUCATION**

P.O. Box 944272

721 Capitol Mall (95814)

Sacramento, CA 94244-2720

916-657-2451

www.cde.ca.gov

**COLORADO DEPARTMENT OF EDUCATION**

201 East Colfax Avenue

Denver, CO 80203-1799

303-866-6600

www.cde.state.co.us

**CONNECTICUT STATE DEPARTMENT OF EDUCATION**

165 Capitol Avenue

Hartford, CT 06145

860-713-6548

www.state.ct.us/sde

**DELAWARE DEPARTMENT OF EDUCATION**

John G. Townsend Building

401 Federal Street

P.O. Box 1402

Dover, DE 19903-1402

302-739-4601

www.doe.state.de.us

**DISTRICT OF COLUMBIA TEACHER EDUCATION AND LICENSURE BRANCH**

441 Fourth Street, NW, Suite 920 South

Washington, DC 20001

202-727-6436

www.washingtondc.gov/citizen/education.htm

**FLORIDA DEPARTMENT OF EDUCATION**

Turlington Building

325 West Gaines Street

Tallahassee, FL 32399-0400

850-487-1785

www.firn.edu/doe

**GEORGIA DEPARTMENT OF EDUCATION**

205 Jesse Hill Jr. Drive, S.E.

Atlanta, GA 30334

404-656-2800

www.doe.k12.ga.us

**HAWAII DEPARTMENT OF EDUCATION**

P.O. Box 2360

Honolulu, HI 96804

808-586-3230

http://doe.k12.hi.us

**IDAHO DEPARTMENT OF EDUCATION**

650 West State Street

P.O. Box 83720

Boise, ID 83720-0027

208-332-6800

www.sde.state.id.us/Dept

**ILLINOIS DEPARTMENT OF EDUCATION**

100 West Randolph, Suite 14-300

Chicago, IL 60601

312-814-2220

www.isbe.state.il.us

**INDIANA DEPARTMENT OF EDUCATION**

State House, Room 229

Indianapolis, IN 46204-2795

317-232-0808

www.ideanet.doe.state.il.us

**IOWA DEPARTMENT OF EDUCATION**

Grimes State Office Building

Des Moines, IA 50319-0416

515-281-5294

www.state.ia.us/educate

**KANSAS DEPARTMENT OF EDUCATION**

120 Southeast 10th Avenue

Topeka, KS 66612-1182

785-296-3201

www.ksbe.state.ks.us

**KENTUCKY DEPARTMENT OF EDUCATION**

500 Mero Street

Frankfort, KY 40601

502-564-4770

800-533-5372

www.kde.state.ky.us

**LOUISIANA HIGHER EDUCATION AND TEACHING**

626 North 4th Street

P.O.Box 94064

Baton Rouge, LA 70804-9064

225-342-4411

877-453-2721

www.doe.state.la.us

**MAINE DIVISION OF CERTIFICATION AND PLACEMENT**

Department of Education

23 State House Station

Augusta, ME 04333

207-624-6618

www.state.me.us/education/homepage.htm

**MARYLAND STATE DEPARTMENT OF EDUCATION**

200 West Baltimore Street

Baltimore, MD 21201

410-767-0100

www.msde.state.md.us

**MASSACHUSETTS DEPARTMENT OF EDUCATION**

350 Main Street

Malden, MA 02148-5023

781-338-3000

www.doe.mass.edu

**MICHIGAN DEPARTMENT OF EDUCATION**

608 West Allegan Street

Hannah Building

Lansing, MI 43933

517-373-3324

www.mde.state.mi.us

**MINNESOTA DEPARTMENT OF CHILDREN, FAMILIES, AND LEARNING**

1500 Highway 36 West

Roseville, MN 55113

651-582-8200

www.educ.state.mn.us

**MISSISSIPPI DEPARTMENT OF EDUCATION**

Central High School

P.O. Box 771

359 North West Street

Jackson, MS 39205

601-359-3513

www.mde.k12.ms.us

**MISSOURI DEPARTMENT OF ELEMENTARY AND SECONDARY EDUCATION**

P.O. Box 480

Jefferson City, MO 65102

573-751-4212

www.mde.k12.ms.us

**MONTANA OFFICE OF PUBLIC INSTRUCTION**

P.O. Box 202501

Helena, MT 59620-2501

406-444-3150

www.opi.state.mt.us

**NEBRASKA DEPARTMENT OF EDUCATION**

301 Centennial Mall South

Lincoln, NE 68509

402-471-2295

www.nde.state.ne.us

**NEVADA DEPARTMENT OF EDUCATION**

700 East Fifth Street

Carson City, NV 89701-5096

775-687-9200

www.nde.state.nv.us

**NEW HAMPSHIRE DEPARTMENT OF
EDUCATION**

101 Pleasant Street

Concord, NH 03301-3860

603-271-3494

www.ed.state.nh.us

**NEW JERSEY DEPARTMENT OF EDUCATION**

P.O. Box 500

100 Riverview Place

Trenton, NJ 08625-0500

609-292-4469

www.state.nj.us/education

**NEW MEXICO DEPARTMENT OF
EDUCATION**

Licensure Unit

Education Building

300 Don Gaspar

Santa Fe, NM 87501-2786

505-827-6516

http://sde.state.nm.us

**NEW YORK STATE EDUCATION
DEPARTMENT**

Education Building

89 Washington Avenue

Albany, NY 12234

518-474-5844

www.nysed.gov

**NORTH CAROLINA STATE DEPARTMENT OF
PUBLIC INSTRUCTION**

301 North Wilmington Street

Raleigh, NC 27601-2825

919-807-3300

www.dpi.state.nc.us

**NORTH DAKOTA EDUCATION STANDARDS
AND PRACTICES BOARD**

600 East Boulevard Avenue, Department 201

Floors 9, 10, & 11

Bismark, ND 58505-0440

701-328-2260

www.dpi.state.nd.us

**OHIO DEPARTMENT OF EDUCATION**

Teacher Education and Certification and Professional
 Development

25 South Front Street

Columbus, OH 43215-4183

877-772-7771

www.ode.state.oh.us

**OKLAHOMA STATE DEPARTMENT OF
EDUCATION**

2500 North Lincoln Blvd.

Oklahoma City, OK 73105-4599

405-521-3301

http://sde.state.ok.us/home

**OREGON DEPARTMENT OF EDUCATION**

255 Capitol Street NE

Salem, OR 97310-0203

503-378-3569

www.ode.state.or.us

**PENNSYLVANIA DEPARTMENT OF
EDUCATION**

333 Market Street

Harrisburg, PA 17126-0333

717-783-6788

www.pde.psu.edu

**RHODE ISLAND DEPARTMENT OF EDUCATION**

255 Westminster Street

Providence, RI 02903

401-222-4600

www.ridoe.net

**SOUTH CAROLINA DEPARTMENT OF EDUCATION**

Rutledge Building

1429 Senate Street

Columbia, SC 29201

803-734-8815

www.sde.state.sc.us

**SOUTH DAKOTA DEPARTMENT OF EDUCATION**

Kneip Building, 3rd Floor

700 Governors Drive

Pierre, SD 57501-2291

605-773-3134

www.state.sd.us/deca

**TENNESSEE STATE DEPARTMENT OF EDUCATION**

Andrew Johnson Tower, 6th Floor

710 James Robertson Parkway

Nashville, TN 37243-0375

617-741-2731

www.state.tn.us/education

**TEXAS EDUCATION AGENCY**

William B. Travis Building

1701 North Congress Avenue

Austin, TX 78701-1494

512-463-9734

www.tea.state.tx.us

**UTAH STATE OFFICE OF EDUCATION**

250 East 500 South

Salt Lake City, UT 84111

801-538-7500

www.usoe.k12.ut.us

**VERMONT DEPARTMENT OF EDUCATION**

120 State Street

Montpelier, VT 05620-2501

802-828-3135

www.state.vt.us/educ

**VIRGINIA DEPARTMENT OF EDUCATION**

P.O. Box 2120

Richmond, VA 23218

800-292-3820

www.pen.k12.va.us

**WASHINGTON DEPARTMENT OF EDUCATION**

Old Capitol Building

P.O. Box 47200

Olympia, WA 98504-7200

360-725-6000

www.k12.wa.us

**WEST VIRGINIA DEPARTMENT OF EDUCATION**

1900 Kanawha Boulevard East

Charleston, WV 25305

304-558-2681

http://wvde.state.wv.us

**WISCONSIN DEPARTMENT OF PUBLIC INSTRUCTION**

P.O. Box 7841

125 South Webster Street

Madison, WI 53707

800-441-4563

www.dpi.state.wi.us

**WYOMING DEPARTMENT OF EDUCATION**

2300 Capitol Avenue

Hathaway Building, 2nd Floor

Cheyenne, WY 82002-0050

307-777-7675

www.k12.wy.us

# Resources For Parents

## Websites for Parents of Children with Special Needs

High States Graduation Testing and Children with Learning Disabilities: www.ldonline.org/ld_indepth/assessment/oneill.html

Visit also the Council for Exceptional Children at: www.cec.sped.org/bk/cectoday/2000/highstakes_sept2000.html

And for a discussion of the impact of high stakes testing on alternative schools, see: www.psych.rochester.edu/SDT/cont_testing.html

## An Excellent General Website

www.hbem.com/library/parents.htm

## Websites for Math Resources

www.mathgoodies.com/parents.shtm

www.ed.gov/pubs/parents/math

www.web.math.fsu.edu/science/education.htm

www.a0kteacherstuff.com/math_resources.htm


## Websites for English/Language Arts Resources

www.eduplace.com/parents/rdg

www.school.discovery.com/schrockguide/arts/artlit.html

www.teams.lacoe.edu/documentation/places/language.html

www.dpi.state.wi.us/dpi/dlsis/cal/calteapr.html


## Additional Essays and Articles Discussing High Stakes Testing

From *Education Week*, the national newspaper devoted to news and issues relating to educational issues in our nation's public schools, the following is a must read article in defense of national testing:

www.educationnews.org/in_defense_of_testing_series_uni.htm

Many researchers and professional organizations are very wary of high stakes testing. See what the *National Education Association* has to say at:

www.nea.org/issues/high-stakes

Compare the National Education Association position with the following from Harvard University's *Civil Rights Project*:

www.law.harvard.edu/groups/civilrights/conferences/testing98/drafts/
natriello99.html

Then go to the *National Board on Educational Testing and Public Policy* and see what it has to say:

http://nbetpp.bc.edu/statements/V1N3.pdf

Read what the nation's chief school officers say about testing in a series of articles on the *American Association of School Administrators* website:

www.aasa.org/publications/sa/2000_12/contents.htm

See what the *National Association of Elementary School Principals* says:
www.naesp.org/comm/c0200.htm

The list of websites could go on and on. High stakes testing is a hot topic in educational research today. Sign on to any good search engine and read away!

## Start Helping Your Child Today

You've heard this before, and it's true. The most effective means of improving your child's literacy skills is to encourage reading. Following is a grade-by-grade list of suggested books. It is important to note that developing readers enjoy reading books by the same authors; that's why series books are encouraged.

## Books for Pre-K and Kindergarten

*Chick Chicka Boom Boom* by Bill Martin Jr.

*Clifford, the Big Red Dog* (and others in the series) by Norman Bridwell

*The Very Hungry Caterpillar* by Eric Carle

*The Grouchy Ladybug* by Eric Carle

*Freight Train* by Donald Crews

*Chester's Way* by Kevin Henkes

*Owen* by Kevin Henkes

*Baby Duck* (and others in the series) by Amy Hest

*Exactly the Opposite* by Tana Hoban

*Brown Bear, Brown Bear, What Do You See?* by Bill Martin, Jr.

*Jelly Beans for Sale* by Bruce McMillan

*Little Bear* (and others in the series) by Else Holmelund Minark

*There Was an Old Lady Who Swallowed a Fly* by Simms Taback

*Pearl Plants a Tree* by Jane Breskin Zalben

*I Lost My Tooth* by Hans Wilhelm

*Berenstain Bears* (series) by Stan and Jan Berenstain

*Clifford Books* (series) by Norman Bridwell

*Curious George Books* (series) by Margaret and H.A. Rey

*Madeline* books (series) by Ludwig Bemelmans

*Minerva Louise* by Janet Morgan Stoeke

*Amelia Bedelia* (series) by Peggy Parish
*Nate The Great* (series) by Marjorie Sharmat
*Boxcar Children* (series) by Gertrude Warner
*Frog and Toad* (series) by Arnold Lobel
*Alison's Wings* by Marion Dane Bauer
*The Mitten* by Jan Brett
*Golly Sisters Go West* by Betsy Byars
*The Very Clumsy Click Beetle* by Eric Carle
*Video Shop Sparrow* by Joy Cowley
*The Baby Dances* by Kathy Henderson
*Hush Little Alien* by Daniel Kirk
*Grandmother Bryant's Pocket* by Jacqueline Briggs Martin
*Zack's Alligator* by Shirley Mozelle
*The Paperboy* by Dav Pilkey
*Where the Wild Things Are* by Maurice Sendak
*Morris the Moose* by Bernard Wiseman
*Danny and the Dinosaur* by Syd Hoff

## Second Grade

*The Gingerbread Man* by Jim Aylesworth
*Willy the Wizard* by Anthony Browne
*Fanny's Dream* by Caralyn Buehner
*The Magic School Bus* by Joanna Cole
*Ramona* (series) by Beverly Cleary
*Stellaluna* by Janell Cannon
*Tikki Tikki Tembo* by Arlene Mosel
*The Stinky Cheeseman and Other Fairly Stupid Fairy Tales* by Jon Scieszka

## Third Grade

*The Great Brain* (series) by John Fitzgerald
*Little House on the Prairie* (series) by Laura Ingalls Wilder
*The Baby Sitters Club* (series) by Ann Martin

*Ramona* (series) by Beverly Cleary
*Anastasia Krupnik* (series) by Lois Lowry
*Stories Julian Tells* by Ann Cameron
*Miss Rumphius* by Barbara Cooney
*The Gruffalo* by Julia Donaldson
*Miss Alaineus: A Vocabulary Disaster* by Debra Frasier
*Lunchroom of Doom* by Daniel Pinkwater
*Misty of Chincoteague* by Marguerite Henry
*Knights of the Kitchen Table* by Jon Scieszka
*Tales of a Fourth Grade Nothing* by Judy Blume

## Fourth Grade

*Help! I'm a Prisoner in the Library* by Eth Clifford
*Amber Brown* (series) by Paula Danziger
*Fourth Grade Wizards* by Barthe DeClements
*26 Fairmount Avenue* (series) by Tomie DePaola
*Half Magic* by Edward Eager
*Music of Dolphins* by Karen Hesse
*Adventures of Ali Baba Bernstein* by Johanna Hurwitz
*James and the Giant Peach* by Roald Dahl
*Stuart Little* by E.B. White
*The Indian in the Cupboard* by Lynne Reid Banks
*The Courage of Sarah Noble* by Alice Dalgliesh

## Fifth Grade

*Julie* by Jean Craighead George
*Julie of the Wolves* by Jean Craighead George
*Shadow Spinner* by Susan Fletcher
*If You're Not Here, Please Raise Your Hand* by Kalli Dakos
*Lincoln: A Photobiography* by Russell Freedman
*Where the Red Fern Grows* by Wilson Rawls
*Bridge to Terabithia* by Katherine Paterson
*Tuck Everlasting* by Natalie Babbitt
*Maniac Magee* by Jerry Spinelli

## Sixth Grade

*Number the Stars* by Lois Lowry
*The Cay* by Theodore Tail
*The Westing Game* by Ellen Raskin
*Bud, Not Buddy* by Christopher Paul Curtis
*The View from Saturday* by E.L. Konigsburg
*The Magic Finger* by Roald Dahl
*The Summer of the Swans* by Betsy Byars
*Island of the Blue Dolphins* by Scott O'Dell
*Black Beauty* by Anna Sewell
*Bat 6* by Virginia Euwer
*Anne of Green Gables* (series) by L.M. Montgomery
*The Ballad of Lucy Whipple* by Karen Cushman
*A Wrinkle in Time* by Madeline L'Engle
*The Cat Ate My Gymsuit* by Paula Danziger
*Treasure Island* by R.L. Stevenson
*Wringer* by Jerry Spinelli
*Crazy Lady* by Jane Lesley Conly

## Seventh Grade

*Slave Dancer* by Paula Fox
*Here's to You, Rachel Robinson* by Judy Blume
*The Outsiders* by S.E. Hinton
*The Pigman* by Paul Zindel
*The Haymeadow* by Gary Paulsen
*Bull Run* by Paul Fleischman
*Shabanu: Daughter of the Wind* by Suzanne Fisher Staples
*The Devil's Arithmetic* by Jane Yolen
*The Pistachio Prescription* by Paula Danziger
*Fantastic Voyage* by Isaac Asimov
*Dandelion Wine* by Ray Bradbury
*The True Confessions of Charlotte Doyle* by Avi

# Eighth Grade

*Nothing But the Truth* by Avi
*Whirligig* by Paul Fleischman
*California Blue* by David Klass
*Cold Sassy Tree* by Olive Ann Burns
*Earthquake at Dawn* by Kristiana Gregory
*Rumble Fish* by S.E. Hinton
*A Hero Ain't Nothin' But a Sandwich* by Alice Childress
*Out of the Dust* by Karen Hesse
*Summer of My German Soldier* by Bette Green
*Zlata's Diary* by Zlata Filipovic
*The Ramsay Scallop* by Frances Temple
*Dicey's Song* by Cynthia Voight

# Magazines for Children that Make Great Birthday Presents and Holiday Gifts

- ▶ *American Girl*
- ▶ *Cricket*
- ▶ *Jack and Jill*
- ▶ *Muse*
- ▶ *National Geographic World*
- ▶ *Ranger Rick*
- ▶ *Sports Illustrated for Kids*
- ▶ *Time Magazine for Kids*

# Ninth through Twelfth Grades

At this level most good adult novels are appropriate. Students should be reading for pleasure and choosing from a variety of nonfiction and fiction. Suggestions include biographies, autobiographies, novels, short stories, and essays. The following is a list of some classics often assigned in school, but they certainly can be read independently as well.

*The Sun Also Rises* by Ernest Hemingway
*To Kill A Mockingbird* by Harper Lee
*The Heart Is a Lonely Hunter* by Carson McCullers
*The Chosen* by Chaim Potok
*A Tree Grows in Brooklyn* by Betty Smith
*In Cold Blood* by Truman Capote
*Animal Farm* by George Orwell
*A Tale of Two Cities* by Charles Dickens
*The Awakening* by Kate Chopin
*Call of the Wild* by Jack London
*Catcher in the Rye* by J.D. Salinger
*The Crucible* by Arthur Miller
*David Copperfield* by Charles Dickens
*Death of a Salesman* by Arthur Miller
*Diary of a Young Girl* by Anne Frank
*Fahrenheit 451* by Ray Bradbury
*The Illustrated Man* by Ray Bradbury
*Black Boy* by Richard Wright
*Invisible Man* by Ralph Ellison
*The Grapes of Wrath* by John Steinbeck
*The Great Gatsby* by F. Scott Fitzgerald
*Huckleberry Finn* by Mark Twain
*I Know Why the Caged Bird Sings* by Maya Angelou
*Jane Eyre* by Charlotte Bronte
*Johnny Got His Gun* by Dalton Trumbo
*The Joy Luck Club* by Amy Tan
*Portrait of the Artist as a Young Man* by James Joyce
*Pride and Prejudice* by Jane Austen
*Red Badge of Courage* by Stephen Crane
*Slaughterhouse Five* by Kurt Vonnegut

## Last, but not Least, There's an Excellent Website for Vocabulary Enrichment

www.vocabulary.com/classic.html